COURAGE
and a Castle

A Wood Dragon Book

COURAGE
and a Castle

A Tribute To A Remarkable Woman

W.J. Koczka

A Wood Dragon Book

Courage and a Castle
A Tribute to a Remarkable Woman
Copyright © 2025 Wanita J. Koczka

This book is a creative non-fiction memoir. It reflects the author's present recollections of experiences over a period of years. All rights reserved. With the exception of brief quotations in book reviews, no part of this publication may be reproduced in any form whatsoever without the permission of the publisher or author. No part of this book may be used or reproduced in any manner for the purpose of training artificial intelligence technologies or systems.

ISBN: 978-1-990863-974 Hardcover
ISBN: 978-1-990863-967 eBook
ISBN: 978-1-990863-950 Paperback

Cover Design: Yago Domingues
Interior Design: Christine Lee
Front/back cover photos: front (Mary Koczka), back cover (Wanita and Mary Koczka)
Photos of Bessborough Hotel - Old Canada Series
https://oldcanada.ca/about

Published by: Wood Dragon Books
Post Office Box 429
Mossbank, Saskatchewan, Canada S0H3G0
www.wooddragonbooks.com

To contact the publisher: wooddragonbooks@gmail.com
To contact the author: wjkoczka@outlook.com
For more information about the book:
https://linktr.ee/Courage.and.a.Castle

Contents

Prologue	1
The Man in Red	5
The Lord is My Shepherd	16
Life's New Path	24
Growing and Adapting	31
The Castle On The River	40
Foundations and Family Loss	62
The Family Move	77
Vexed Vision	103
Birthday Slippers	112
Turbulent Times	119
The Christmas Miracle	137
You Are My Sunshine	153
Shades of Mary	167
The Anniversary Road Trip	176
An Angel for Mary	191
Hospital	207
Home to the Acreage	236
Heaven	254
Gifts From Mom	266
Epilogue - May: The Month of Mary	283
Acknowledgements	293
About the Author	295

Dedication

To my mother, Mary,
thank you for sharing your wisdom,
providing gentle nudging and guidance, and,
most of all, for your unconditional love.

Even in your earthly absence,
you continue to support and inspire me.

Love You, Miss You, God Bless You

Prologue

I wrote this book, a rich tapestry, from my heart — to celebrate and honour the remarkable life of my mother, Mary Elizabeth Koczka (nee Brecht). My mother was an extraordinary woman ahead of her time; a role model and an inspiration for me, my family, and many others who had the pleasure of knowing her.

In March 2020, just as the COVID-19 pandemic hit and fundamentally changed the way we existed in the world, I retired. I was sixty-eight, the same age as Mom when she retired. Mom, ninety-six at the beginning of the pandemic, was in a private personal care home in Prince Albert, about 25 minutes from my acreage. Although she had lived in Saskatoon most of her adult years, a life-altering event made it necessary for her to be in a seniors' home. The family decided that, as I was her primary caregiver, she should live closer to me.

One of the things I planned to do once I retired was to spend more time with Mom. Despite having limited mobility and being diagnosed with Alzheimer's, she was healthy and still enjoyed coming to my acreage and going on outings. These outings could no longer occur once quarantine was initiated. Older people were particularly vulnerable to the virus. As a result, Mother could not leave the care home or even her room for many months and was isolated for the last year of her life.

However, in late April 2021, after a fall and a brief stay in the hospital, a doctor advised us that Mom's condition could result in her living only for a few more months, or even just a few more days. She was designated palliative care, and my sisters and I were honoured to care for her the last few days of her well-lived life. She died on May 5, 2021, in my home on our acreage.

My family and I found the loss of our mother, the family matriarch, heart-wrenching and difficult to process. We were not ready to be motherless.

Without my mom and her needs as the focus for my time and energy — I was lost. Emotionally, I was devastated. Yet, in the face of my profound loss, I found the strength to carry on with the wisdom and teachings Mom had shared.

Christmas 2021 was nearing. I was not looking forward to Christmas without Mom, who loved Christmas. Her love for this holiday had always been the heart of our family traditions. Slowly, through December, it became more apparent that Mom was nudging me to spend my time writing. I had always said, one day, I would write. As to what to write, it became clear I should write about Mom's life and the impact she had on me and our family.

My grief guided me to the events of my mother's life that were vital and memorable. I have narrated them for you in this memoir. I anticipate these stories which explore the human condition through the lens of my mother's life, will resonate with your heartstrings and sense of humour. I invite you to share my mother's journey and hope you come to know and love my mother as our family did.

The Man in Red

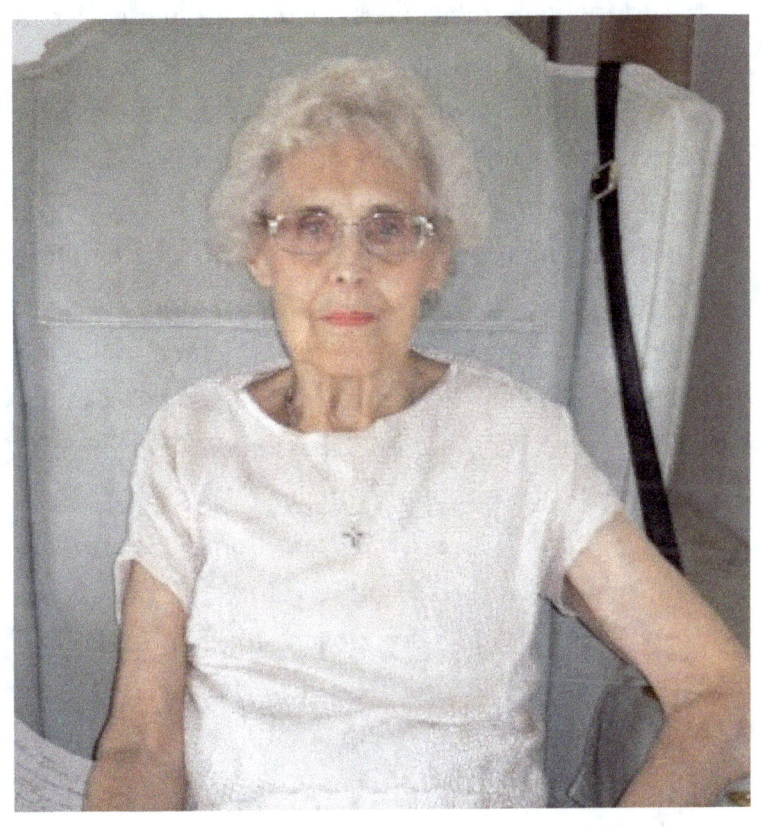

Mary Koczka
2008

COURAGE AND A CASTLE

In the last year, I have often spoken about The Man in Red to the staff and my family members. "The Man in Red was here today," I would say. When he visits, he always tells me, "I have loved you since the first moment I saw you." I feel so loved, special, and safe when he visits.

My daughter, who lives nearby, always looks perplexed when I tell her the Man in Red has come to visit. The staff at my personal care home are also confused as to who this imaginary person might be that dominates my thoughts.

I am now ninety-seven years old. In 2013, when I was ninety, I suffered a brain bleed and survived the surgery to remedy it. I was honoured with the distinction of being called the family's "Christmas Miracle." I have continued as the family matriarch, to my delight and to that of my family.

After surgery, I moved from Saskatoon, where I had lived all my life, to a care home in Prince Albert to be closer to my daughter, my only child living in the province. I am content living here.

My balance is a bit off now, so I am supervised when I use my walker to move around. I am taken in a wheelchair for longer distances. Almost daily, I pray with my son over the phone. I love to play bingo and attend church services with other residents, play "find-a-word" on my tablet, listen to music — especially polka music — and sing along with the groups that come to the care home. Sometimes, I sing "You are My Sunshine" with the staff.

I am well taken care of. On Mondays, the hairdresser washes, sets, and styles my hair. My fingernails are freshly polished every Friday, and my feet massaged every few weeks. My life extends beyond the facility. I enjoy going to the casino for supper and playing the machines with my daughters. Often, I win, and that makes me smile.

My family often include me in vacations and sports events. Sometimes we just spend time together as a family. In these past few years, I haven't gone much further than my daughter's acreage or the lake, or back and forth to Saskatoon or Prince Albert with my daughter for appointments. My age is catching up with me and I no longer have the energy I did when I was younger.

I am always up for an adventure and willing to try new things. Staff at the care home call me their "social butterfly." I am always grateful to welcome another day. I believe in God, have unlimited faith, and love my family unconditionally. My children sometimes affectionately refer to me as "Holy Mary" and their children fondly call me "Little Gram" or "Grandma Mary."

My short-term memory isn't that good anymore. In the past, my daughter would ask me what I had for supper, and I would tell her roast beef and gravy with mashed potatoes, carrots, and cake for dessert. It was a favourite meal as I liked those foods — especially mashed potatoes and gravy. More recently, though, when she asks me what I have eaten, I say, "I don't remember, but I know I ate because they always feed me." My daughter no longer asks me what I have eaten; maybe she knows I can't remember. Alzheimer's is affecting my life, and I struggle to understand daily activities and remember my past. I have brief spells of absolute clarity but most of the time I live in the moment, a small world of "now." But whenever the Man In Red visits me, I remember my past and I travel back to a time of hope, health, and love.

I grew up in a German farming household near Carmel, Saskatchewan and my first language was German. As a result, I knew very little English when I started school. I was the second oldest of eleven children so I helped my father with chores and farming until my younger brothers were older and strong enough to do the work. I liked working hard and helping others.

School was challenging for me. I liked to learn but often missed school during harvest and seeding seasons. After missing a month or more, I found it difficult to understand the content the class was working on and could not catch up on the lessons I had missed. I had to be satisfied with learning what I could while I was in class.

Our family attended Sunday mass as frequently as the weather would allow. My father would lead the family in praying the Rosary every Sunday night before bed, with all of our family members kneeling, our rosaries in hand. I always enjoyed praying the Rosary. The word rosary means a chain of roses, and the roses are prayers. Saying the "Lord's Prayer" and the "Hail Mary" on the rosary calmed me, connected me to my faith through prayer and to God through the Virgin Mary, providing me with peace and guidance throughout my life.

I went to work at age fifteen, as my father decided and arranged. I had not yet completed Grade Eight. I was slight in build and just barely five feet tall, but I was strong from working on the farm. I was a shy and reserved girl with jet-black hair and bright blue eyes. My first job was working for my uncle, close to our family farm. Later, I went to work in another community, where I met Johnny, my husband-to-be.

Johnny was one of seven children and had also grown up on a farm near Viscount. His parents were Hungarian and the family spoke Hungarian at home as well as English. John helped with chores, seeding, and harvesting. He was mechanically gifted, which was helpful, as his father was not so inclined. However, both father and son were thinkers. They would approach problems in a methodical manner, analyzing options, and creating solutions in a way that others could not.

John attended school about half a mile from his farm and completed Grade Nine. As a young man, he would ride horses bareback and train them to do tricks. He was a daredevil at heart. He was very fit, lean, and muscular due to his work on the farm. He wore his thick dark brown hair slicked back; his deep brown eyes held a hint of mischief and he was quick to flash a broad, white-toothed smile. His eastern European ancestry showed, with his large ear lobes, olive-coloured skin, and medium height.

His family home was a welcome hub for visiting with family and friends, with activities accompanied by drinking, smoking, and wonderful food. Singing, dancing, and playing musical instruments were integral to visits. Growing up, he learned to play the fiddle, accordion, mouth organ, and the spoons. He inherited his love of dancing from his mother and father — and could he dance! He also loved to sing; his deep voice could be heard harmonizing with others as he expressed emotion through hand gestures and facial expressions.

Johnny took pride in looking good and dressing

smartly. His sisters would press his shirts, suit jacket, and pants in exchange for him driving them to dances in the community. He walked sure-footed and straight-backed, his head held high, ready to warmly greet people.

When he went to work after Grade Nine, he found employment at his uncle's garage in Viscount. Johnny developed his mechanical skills further and soon he could fix almost anything.

He and his brother, Mike Jr., both received certificates of medical unfitness for enrollment in the army in June of 1942 due to flat footedness. Early during the war, they travelled to Ontario where they worked in a John Deere plow manufacturing plant for a time, but eventually found the weather and the inside work did not suit them. From there, they crossed back to Saskatchewan, spent a few months at the family farm and then headed to Prince George, British Columbia, where Johnny worked at the Canadian National Railway in a roundhouse as a boilermaker helper. The rainy climate did not suit the two brothers so they returned to the family farm. Johnny later worked in Regina on steam engines and boilers and a few other pursuits before resuming work at his uncle's garage.

It was around 1943 that I first met Johnny; I had noticed him at community dances and would dance with him if he asked me. All the girls wanted to dance with the "Handsome Hungarian."

I was working for a family, helping with daily household chores. In the evening, I took sewing classes with my girlfriends. After sewing class, we would go to the local café and Johnny would often be there. He would play the Wurlitzer — the café jukebox — singing along to the song and dancing with whoever was there. He would encourage others to get up and dance and would serenade them as the songs played. He was good-looking, entertaining, and fun to watch.

Coincidentally, Johnny was responsible for keeping the furnace going in the building where I took my sewing classes. One evening, he asked if he could walk me home, and I agreed. We stopped in at the local café on the way, and he sang along to the music, and we danced. After that, Johnny would wait for me after each sewing class and walk me home. My heart would race when he held my hand; I never felt like this before. I thought I was falling in love.

Once sewing classes ended, we would see each other at dances, and he would ask me to dance. I always said, "Yes." We both loved to dance and danced so well together.

When I was young, July 1, or Dominion Day as it was called back then, was a day of celebration. Most towns held what they called "Sports Day" which had a carnival-like atmosphere with races, competitions, games, food, and an evening dance. All the townsfolk and countryfolk would spend the day celebrating and enjoying each other's company. It was at the dance in the evening that Johnny asked me to be his girlfriend. My heart nearly exploded. I was so excited and proud to be the girlfriend of the Handsome Hungarian.

Months later, when we were at the wedding dance of a friend of Johnny's, he proposed to me. I vividly remember his dark navy suit, red tie, and red rose boutonniere. We danced a waltz and then he took my hand and led me outside. He gently took the red rose from his lapel and set it in my dark hair. Softly and earnestly, he said, "I have loved you since the first moment I saw you. I will love you forever and I will look after you forever. Mary, will you marry me and be my wife forever?"

He bent forward and softly kissed me. I melted in his arms and whispered, "Yes, I will marry you, and I will love you forever and be your wife forever."

In March of 1945, Johnny declared that, between the two of us, we had saved enough money to have a wedding and set up a house together. We married on April 14, 1945, in Viscount, the town where we both worked. I felt beautiful in the fitted, white-lattice wedding dress I had purchased. John looked like the handsome Hungarian I fell in love with, in his black suit with a red tie and red rose boutonniere. I was marrying the Handsome

Hungarian. I was so in love and so proud. What a perfect day it was!

The day after the wedding, we set off to Saskatoon for a honeymoon. As newlyweds, we stayed at a fancy hotel for one night and then spent a few days with a family friend. Those were some of the happiest days of my life.

Then it was time to go back to work. Johnny decided that if we both worked on the same farm, we could have housing and jobs together, so we found work with a farmer in the Viscount area; however, once seeding was completed, the farmer did not want to pay us. So, in early summer, we moved to Saskatoon, where we purchased a small house and both found work at St. Paul's Hospital. We walked to and from work together, hand-in-hand, smiling, talking, laughing, and singing. People would remark what a happy and in-love couple we were. We were delighted to be in love and married to one another. I was living the bountiful life of love and happiness I had only imagined.

Now, at ninety-seven years old, I sit in my high-backed Bessborough Hotel chair in my comfortable room in the care home. My once jet-black hair is a natural silver and has been beautifully groomed by the hairdresser. My nails are polished a bright red. I have red rouge on my cheeks that is not blended in as much as it should be and my lips are coloured with my favorite red lipstick. My family say my skin is beautiful, soft, clear, and almost wrinkle-free. The caregiving staff helped me dress in black pants and a red sweater with gold sequins. Zoey, my caregiver, carefully positioned a flower in my hair, a red rose from the bouquet beside my bed. I love flowers, especially red roses. One of my daughters sends me flowers weekly. My daughters say I look beautiful, like a refined, wealthy lady. I am ready for the day, and I am grateful.

I am surrounded by mementos of my life, photos of my family, and a picture of Johnny and I on our wedding day seventy-six years ago. I still listen to the waltzes and polkas that Johnny and I used to dance to. The music makes my heart happy, and I tap my toes to the beat. When I get up to walk with my walker, I keep beat to the music as I step along, still loving to dance. I miss Johnny and yearn to be with him again. When he comes to visit, he wears the same dark navy suit, red tie, and red rose boutonniere he wore the night he proposed.

I told my family that the Man in Red visited me today. I am so happy when he comes to visit, even though my family tells me he has been dead for over 40 years. Maybe the next time Johnny visits, I will dance away in his arms where I will feel loved, safe, and special.

The Lord is My Shepherd

**Mary Brecht and John Koczka
on their Wedding Day**
April 14, 1945

According to all accounts, the first year of my parents' marriage was blissful. Shortly after their wedding in 1945, Mom and Dad moved to Saskatoon where they both found work at St. Paul's Hospital. Their jobs offered them financial stability and the opportunity for my dad to pursue a career in the stationery engineer trade. Working together and planning for the birth of their first child was more wonderful than they had imagined. In the evenings, they shared their dreams with each other — my mother hoped to have a large family, and my father hoped his apprenticeship would increase his capacity to provide for their future family.

Rose Robbestad (Mary's sister-in-law)
Mary (pregnant with Wesley)
Madeline Hyland (Mary's sister)
Late 1949

COURAGE AND A CASTLE

Money was plentiful, and they had bought a small house. Mom's older sister, Madeline, Dad's sister, Rose, and his brother, Mike, were living with them at the time. Madeline and Rose were best friends and they both worked at Intercontinental Packers. It was a houseful of young people starting out in life. The future ahead for the newlyweds seemed to be very bright.

However, just before their first anniversary, a tragic event changed the course of their lives. Dad was in a life-threatening accident in the laundry area of the hospital. Dad was replacing a part on the industrial mangle, a massive machine that wrung the water out of the laundry. He had almost completed the job when someone accidentally turned the machine on and his right arm was caught in the mangle.

He hung from the mangle, his right arm squashed and twisted between the massive rollers. His bones were shredded from the force of the machine and poked through his flesh; blood gushed from his wounds. The machine was quickly turned off and the massive rollers released Dad's arm.

Mom was working in the kitchen area of the Catholic hospital that day. She heard the sound of alarms followed by announcements over the intercom directing, "All emergency personnel report to the laundry room IMMEDIATELY." Emergency personnel, including doctors, rushed past the kitchen area to the laundry with grave looks on their faces. Mom knew something terrible was happening and Dad might be in danger. Within a few minutes, two Sisters quickly ushered her from her workstation in the kitchen to the kitchen office where they informed her that her husband had been injured.

One nun spoke gently but firmly, "Mary, you must stay with us and let the people trained for emergencies look after Johnny. We will tell you what is happening when we have the information."

"I need to see Johnny; I need to go to him right now!" Mom wailed, her tears streaming down her face. Her heart was racing, her eyes refused to focus, and her mind was playing all sorts of scenarios as to what was happening regarding her husband.

The other Sister reached out and guided Mom's trembling body close to hers, her crucifix and beads pressing into Mom as she wrapped her arms tightly around the crying woman. They swayed quietly from side to side as the Sister gently patted her. "There, there, Mary, with the grace of God, Johnny will be alright."

They brought her tea and tried to comfort her, but Mom continued to weep uncontrollably. Nothing the Sisters said or did brought her comfort. When Madeline and Rose were informed about the accident, they quickly came to the hospital where they were ushered to the kitchen office to be with Mom. Upon seeing her, they too hugged and rocked her, and they all wept until there were no more tears, only involuntary throat noises of anguish and sorrow. With Mom in the company of family, the nuns took the opportunity to leave and gather information to share with Mom.

Once the area of the accident was clear and Dad had been taken to surgery, the Sisters returned to provide an update on the accident. Dad had been placed on a hospital stretcher, his condition assessed, and treatment begun. After briefly speaking with the doctors, he passed out from the pain. The Sisters said that the doctors had told Dad that his arm should be amputated, but before he lost consciousness, he said he would not allow them to remove it. Therefore, he was now going into surgery where the surgeons would try to save his mangled arm. The Sisters advised Mom that it would be a lengthy and complicated surgery, but that she could see Dad once he was in recovery.

With the whole story revealed to them, Mom, Madeline and Rose began to cry again, fearing the worst. The Sisters again offered hugs and prayers and then took the three women to a private waiting room where a Father welcomed them. Together, they prayed special prayers and then prayed the Rosary for Dad. After prayers, Mom and Madeline and Rose hugged one another and began to weep again. Finally, they were convinced to have some tea and toast, which gave them a boost and a more positive outlook on Dad's condition.

Even though she was with two of her closest family while she waited for news of Dad's surgery, the waiting was very difficult for Mom. Late in the evening, once Dad was in recovery, Mom was finally able to see for herself that her husband was living and breathing. As she entered the room, she gasped and stepped backwards quickly. Tubes were hooked up to his body and connected to several machines. A nursing Sister stood beside him, checking the monitors. Mother stood motionless for a few seconds, then rushed to her husband's bedside.

He was without colour, sheet-like, except for the splotches of blood that dotted his exposed upper body. His face grimaced with pain, and his eyes were tightly closed. His right arm was outstretched and elevated, tied to a bar to keep it immobile. It was wrapped in thick bandages that had been white but were now oozing red.

Despite this view, tears of relief streamed down Mom's face as she kissed Dad's forehead and stroked his thick, disheveled hair. Tear drops slid from her face and dropped on his forehead where her lips had been only a moment before. She thanked God her prayers had been answered and that Dad was alive. She felt blessed to carry on life with him. "Johnny, oh Johnny," she whispered as she wept.

Upon hearing Mom's voice and feeling her warm tears, Dad slowly opened his eyes. Their eyes locked momentarily as if to acknowledge each other's pain. He had no strength to speak but groaned softly and closed his eyes to a more peaceful rest, with his Mary by his side.

Mom believed that Dad had been saved by prayer. This was the event that crystallized her relationship with prayer and God. She was not a fanatical religious person but a humble, quietly wise woman who prayed for guidance and followed the teachings of kindness and compassion almost to a fault. Forever grateful to have her Johnny in her life, she vowed to always be by his side, supporting and loving him unconditionally. And so she did.

(As far as my father's religious views are concerned, he supported our Catholic upbringing and insisted we attend church, but he did not participate. His view of the Church, religion, and life was more pragmatic than my mother's.)

Dad insisted that the doctors attempt to save his arm rather than amputate it. However, he was in severe pain for years, and his crippled arm, patched together with pins and plates, oozed from surgery incisions that did not heal properly. He would suffer through a dozen more surgeries from 1946 to 1951 when, finally, a plastic surgeon reopened, cleaned the infected areas, and closed the wound successfully. That final surgery left his ever-painful and mangled-looking arm more useable than it had been. At that point, he decided that he would not endure any further surgery, leaving him to live with pain the remainder of his life.

Life's New Path

Monica Brecht (Mary's Mother)
Mary (holding Baby Wallace)
John Brecht (Mary's Father)
John
1947

After his injury, Dad remained hospitalized for a month for additional surgery. Mom would stay at the hospital each day after work to visit him. Once he was able to go home, he still had to return to the hospital daily for treatments. It was during this treatment time that Mom discovered that she was pregnant with their first child. These were not the circumstances under which they had expected their first baby to be born. Nevertheless, Mom embraced her pregnancy and looked forward to motherhood. She continued to work, but as Dad was still recovering, he could not. He was very frustrated by the circumstances. He didn't want his pregnant wife to have to work; he should be earning money, and she should be home preparing for the birth of their first child.

On October 17, 1946, while Dad was in St. Paul's Hospital recovering from one of the many surgeries on his mangled arm, Mom gave birth to her firstborn son, Wallace, on a different floor, in the same building. They had planned this to be a joyous special occasion, but the circumstances of Dad's injury had altered their lives. It was heart-wrenching for Mom to realize her dream of becoming a mother while her husband was experiencing excruciating pain from yet another surgery. Nonetheless, they both made the best of welcoming their first baby.

COURAGE AND A CASTLE

Mom's firstborn weighed almost ten pounds, a giant baby for a woman of Mom's diminutive size. She should have had a C-section but was too far along in labour when the doctor realized how large the baby's head was. The newborn was pulled out with forceps, and his head was misshapen for a few days. It was a grueling birth for the baby boy and for Mom, who was very weak from blood loss during the traumatic event.

The following day, when the doctor came to see Mom and her big baby boy, he found the new mother smiling lovingly at her newborn son, who lay peacefully on her chest. The doctor remarked he was surprised to see both of them as he hadn't known if either would survive. Mom was shocked by the comment, as she had no idea that she and her babe were so close to death. After the doctor left, she rubbed the medal of the Virgin Mary she had worn around her neck since Dad's accident, pulled her rosary out from under her pillow, and said a prayer of thanks.

Later that afternoon, Dad was wheeled to Mom's room to meet his firstborn son. He kissed his wife gently as she rose to meet him. Tears of joy cascaded down their cheeks as Mom gently set their baby boy on his lap. Dad cooed softly to his son and hugged him tenderly with his good left arm while Mom smiled with contentment and sheer joy.

She felt so blessed, thankful that her prayers had been answered and that she, her Johnny, and baby Wallace would all live to see another day.

It was a torturous time for Mom as she watched Dad suffer through many surgeries and the pain that continued to haunt him daily. They were ever hopeful that the next surgery would be the one to make Dad's arm more mobile and alleviate his suffering, but that was not the case.

Dad's life was permanently changed. Although he continued to support the family financially, he was unable to maintain full-time employment during the surgery years (1946 to 1951) or full-time employment after 1964. As far as his goal of becoming a stationary engineer, that dream, just like his arm, had been crushed. Over time, he found he could still play the mouth organ, the spoons, and the fiddle in some capacity but not to the standard which he had grown accustomed.

As a woman of faith, Mom remained hopeful that Dad would fully recover and life would return to normal. She supported him emotionally and faced the related challenges with hard work, prayer, faith, and perseverance. During the "surgery years," she showed acceptance of the changes, prayed for guidance, gave thanks for what she had, and, gave her unconditional love to my father; behaviours that would become her pattern throughout her life.

The drastic change in Dad's physical capabilities plagued him. He was a proud man and the fact that he could no longer demonstrate his physical skills and knowledge in work meant he had to take jobs that were less labour intensive and that did not require manual dexterity with both hands. He could not maintain a job and advance within a company as he had to quit his position to have each new surgery and then find another when he recovered enough to work again. After the final surgery, Dad's injury was determined to be permanent and he was granted a small disability pension because the accident had been a workplace incident.

He never fully recovered from his injury and the ever-present, mangled arm was both a stark reminder of a dream lost and a new reality he never came to totally accept. Mom's Johnny was no longer the audacious man he once was. Later, he would sometimes take to "self-medicating," as it is referred to these days, with his drink of choice, wine. Though he was a "give the other person the shirt off your back" kind of man to others, over time, he became less kind to his own family. He was a good man who carried a heavy load and sometimes reacted poorly.

Although Mom would be horrified at my mention of this, it is not a revelation. This was her life with my father, for better or worse, and she always chose to look at the bright side; she was an intrinsic optimist and carried on with faith-filled hope. Her life with my father helped mold and shape her into the remarkable woman she was and whom we loved unconditionally, as she loved our father and her children.

Despite the family's hardships, Mom always spoke fondly of those times. She never thought of herself as a victim. She did not lament what life could have or should have been for her, for Dad, or for our family, if only he had not been injured. She accepted the reality of the situation, prayed for guidance, took necessary action, lived in the now, and looked forward to brighter days. She was always engaged with life, hopeful and grateful. She saw the forced change in their lives as an opportunity, which she accepted and embraced, and then moved forward.

During those years, she never lost faith. She remained committed and devoted to my father, never complaining about the life she led with my father and our family. Nor did my father lament that he had not reached his life's dream of becoming a stationary engineer. Neither were complainers. Both evaluated the circumstances that life brought, adapted and moved forward, my mother more graciously than my father.

Mom maintained we were never poor or without money, even when Dad's paychecks weren't regular. He was resourceful, was good at bartering and trading, and would buy and sell property and make money. Early on, when their family was small, they often had family staying with them, which helped pay the bills. Their farm families occasionally gifted them with produce, meat, and flour, making life easier. Mom became well-versed in being frugal and resourceful with their financial and physical resources. Mom and Dad were a team, leading their growing family.

Growing and Adapting

John
wearing his theatre uniform
1949

COURAGE AND A CASTLE

After the birth of her first child, Wallace, in 1946, Mom stayed home, caring for my father through the "surgery years," looking after the family, and managing the household. One of Dad's jobs after the accident was as a projectionist, usher, and cleaner at the Victory Theatre in downtown Saskatoon. The family of three lived in a huge apartment above the Victory Theatre. As accommodation was provided with Dad's position, they sold their little house.

Mom helped Dad with his duties and she spoke fondly of this period. One story was more outstanding than the rest.

One evening in 1949, Wallace, who was about three at the time, sneaked out of the theatre. There was a friendly dog sitting on the sidewalk. The dog had a collar and a shoelace leash. My brother took the dog by its shoelace leash, and they went for a walk.

He was wandering with the dog when a reporter spotted them and took a picture of them. After talking to the boy, the reporter realized that Wallace was lost, even though the little boy denied the fact. The reporter took my brother and the dog to the police station that was only half a block away. My brother was a chatty little fellow and told the police he lived above the theatre downtown. Just as my brother was telling the police that he was not lost and that he didn't know the dog's name because it was not his dog, my Dad called the station to report that his son was missing.

Wallace
article in the Saskatoon Star Phoenix
1949

Dad hurried to the police station where he found his son sitting on the floor with the dog curled up by his feet. Wallace told his dad he was not lost and asked if he could keep the friendly, mixed-terrier dog. Dad agreed to take the dog home for the night and try and find its owner the following day. Wallace was so excited he danced around Dad and grabbed the shoelace leash and Dad's hand, and they all walked home together.

The next day, the newspaper ran the story titled "Start of High Adventure" with a picture of my brother and the dog. Mom kept the original newspaper clipping and the matching eight by ten, black and white photo the newspaper gave her. She often brought the items out to verify the story. She fondly recalled that same son could be found helping his Dad clean the theatre by eating gum that patrons stuck to the bottom of the seats! This was just one of many adventures her eldest son would imprint in her heart and memory.

From one of the windows in their apartment above the theatre, the family could catch a glimpse of the stately Bessborough Hotel on the bank of the South Saskatchewan River. In off hours, Mom, Dad, and little Wallace often walked to the river bank near the hotel. With a packed lunch and a fishing pole (Dad loved to fish), they would spend the afternoon, fishing and picnicking on the lawn near The Bessborough. One such afternoon, Dad was particularly pleased with himself for his fish catch.

As he and Mom finished their lunch and their son played with yet another stray dog, John teased Mary, "When we have money, we will stay in this magnificent hotel for a weekend and be wined, dined, and pampered — just like royalty and movie stars.

We can even have breakfast in bed. Would you like that, Sweetie Pie?"

Taken aback by John's teasing, but very excited that this might possibly happen, Mary quipped back, "I have always loved this hotel, and if I were a princess, I would live here at The Bessborough, and you could be my prince, and we would live happily forever after."

John, Wallace, and Mary
Bessborough Park
1948

The romantic moment was quickly disrupted when it appeared that Wallace would be tempted to more than play with the stray dog, but before he could be taken for a walk by the animal, Dad gathered him up, laughing.

Following another complicated surgery, Dad could no longer work at the theatre, and the family moved to Dad's parents' farm. It was there that my second brother was born in 1950.

Mary
Brecht Family Farm
1949

Our family had six children and all six children had the same initials, WJK. Dad had a girl's name picked out for his firstborn, but was blessed with a son. He liked the initials WJK so he chose a suitable name, Wallace Joseph, for his firstborn son to match those initials. When the second baby was born, again a son, my father (with my mom's approval) selected a name for a son (Wesley John) and saved the baby girl's name, Wanita Janet, for me, his third child and first daughter.

Wallace, Wesley, Mary (holding Wanita)
Koczka Farm
1953

COURAGE AND A CASTLE

In 1951, the year that I was born, we moved back to Saskatoon and bought a small house. Three more children would be born, and all would have the initials WJK, as Dad thought it was fun. In 1954, Winnifred Joan (WJK4), the fourth child, was born; in 1955, Wanda Jane (WJK5), the fifth child, was born; and in 1957, Wayne James (WJK6), the sixth and final child, was born. Our family was complete. As kids, watching our Mother struggle with our names was always wildly amusing. We knew which one of us she wanted, but we would stand by waiting, grinning, as she called out in frustration, "Whu ... Whu ... Whu ...," trying to figure out which of us she was calling.

When we moved back to the city in 1951, Dad found long-term employment at The Royal Canadian Air Force, cleaning and performing light maintenance duties. With Dad's steady job and income, life normalized and was easier for the family. Around 1952, we moved from the tiny house to a slightly larger one on Avenue O South. We lived modestly, just above poverty. However, Mom's view was that we were not poor; we were blessed. Her life was not without trials and tribulations, but she did not dwell on the hardships — she was genuinely grateful for her life with her Johnny and her family. In typical Mom fashion, she flipped the difficulties, showing appreciation for being able to work through them and taking solace in the lessons and opportunities the difficulty had created.

Winnifred, Wanda, Wanita, Mary, Wayne (in front)
Koczka Farm
1959

The Castle On The River

The Bessborough Hotel

My mother had long admired The Bessborough, as did most of the citizens of Saskatoon. Who would not be inspired by such a castle-like hotel? Built by the Canadian National Railway, the hotel often referred to as "The Bessborough" is a ten-story, national and local landmark with chateau-like towers, spires, and dormers, situated on the banks of the South Saskatchewan River. A revered place of prestige and grandness, it was constructed in Depression-era Saskatoon and was completed in 1932. When construction of the hotel was complete, it was not fully furnished for a further three years due to a shortage of funds. Finally, in all its grandeur, it opened its doors to the public in December 1935. It has been said that the building of The Bessborough was a symbol of hope, a monument to progress and prosperity — a symbol that Saskatoon made it through the great depression and was a thriving prairie city, a destination.

From the time it was built and into the early 1960s, the posh Bessborough was the premier hotel in Saskatoon for elite travelers. It hosted many grand events in its two massive ballrooms, the Battleford Room and the Adam Ballroom, which could each seat more than three hundred guests and boasted high, lofty ceilings with gold-toned plaster relief features and terrazzo floors. Many other smaller, yet charming, meeting rooms were available for more intimate gatherings.

Its third-floor Vice Regal Suite offered five-star, luxury accommodations for people of prestige and great stature, such as prime ministers, celebrities, and heads of state such as King George VI and Queen Elizabeth II. Its two hundred and twenty-five guest rooms were appointed with all the luxury and amenities one would expect to experience in the Bavarian-inspired castle. Its first-class, fine-dining facilities, cultured menu, and formal service rounded out the exquisite experience of a stay at this elegant "Castle on the River."

As the railway was the prime mode of transportation during that time, and the Canadian National Railway owned the hotel, the opulent Bessborough was purposefully set in direct sight of the train station. Train passenger pick-up service occurred daily between the train station and The Bessborough. There was a wooden bridge built over the top of the train station whereby a person could walk over the train tracks and train yards to get from one side of the city to the other. This was a pleasant experience for passengers who chose to take the walk and enjoy the breathtaking view of the city.

For Mom, The Bessborough represented a new foundation for her to build upon. It offered the hope and promise of continued progress for her and our family. Just as The Bessborough's downtown location allowed the hotel to serve as an anchor for the city, as Mom's life unfolded, her employment at The Bessborough would come to serve as an anchor for her and our family.

By 1960, it became clear to my mother that our house was "on the wrong side of the tracks." She wanted her children to have better opportunities and a safer neighbourhood in which to grow up. For her, this meant that our family needed to move to a new house in a different neighbourhood.

Dad was working full-time, but Mom believed that if they were to buy a new home in a better area, she needed to contribute financially for this goal to become a reality. Although caring for her children and husband were priorities, she was always open to, and accepting of, change and willing to do the work to achieve a specific goal.

While Mom planned on returning to work part-time to save money towards a down payment on a new house, she did not know the significance of her decision to re-enter the workforce. She did not expect that Dad's steady employment would be terminated (nor that he would work very little after that termination), and that she would become the primary breadwinner.

So it was that in 1960, when her youngest, Wayne, was three, Mom began to look for employment. Before having a family, she worked, first for farm families doing chores, household tasks, and child minding and then later at the hospital where she worked until the birth of her first child in 1946.

Mom's intuition would often prompt her and she would look at the environment, see how the current situation was impacting her family, find a solution, and work towards that goal. Part of her finding a solution was to ask for guidance through prayer. She always said you cannot pray for "things": you pray for guidance to get you to the "things" you need for yourself and your family. She would say, "You might not get what you asked for, but you get what you need." If, at times, she could not come to a solution for her difficulty after some thought, she would say, "I will leave that alone, leave that out there, and it will come." Once a path was shown to her, she would make a decision to unwaveringly work towards her goal.

The thought of a job interview made Mom terribly nervous. With hope and much prayer, she applied for a job at The Bessborough, the Castle on the River she had always admired. She mustered courage, passed the interview process, and was hired as a casual chambermaid, filling in on short notice. Upon hearing she was hired and excited for the opportunity, she rubbed the Virgin Mary medal she wore in thanks.

As kids, we were astonished that our mom was getting a job. Few mothers in our Saskatoon community worked at that time. We worried — what would life be like with Mom going to work? Who would look after us, especially Wayne, who was only three?

Mom's first day in training was full of excitement and awe. As she entered the employee's entrance, she recalled the day many years before in Bessborough Park when Johnny had told her that one day they would spend a weekend at the magnificent hotel and be treated like royalty. So far, that had not happened, but she was always hopeful that maybe one day .... She smiled, remembering that she had told him that if she were a princess, they would live there, and he would be her prince, and they would live happily ever after.

Now here she was, her first day of work, inside the Bessborough Hotel — a farm girl, a wife, and mother of six children, being shown the magnificent front entrance and massive front desk, the elegant ballrooms and fancy dining rooms, the luxury hotel rooms and the impressive Vice Regal suite, as well as the behind-the-scenes state-of-the-art kitchen, service areas, and back stairs. She marveled at the elevator operators and doormen there to greet the exclusive clientele. She felt blessed and honoured to learn about her role at the grand hotel. For her, it was like a dream come true. And it meant she could work towards her goal: saving for a down payment for a new house for her family.

When she came home from her first day at work, she got off the bus stop near my aunt's house, where she had left our youngest brother. When he saw her, he clung to her, weeping. She bent down to wipe his tears and cradle him in her arms. She sat him on her lap, cuddled and stroked him as she told her sister about her first day at work. He wept silently, his little body cringing and shuddering as he tried to gain control of his aching heart. Finally, he was comforted enough to walk home with Mom, his still-trembling, little hand holding hers.

"I don't want you to go to work anymore," he blurted out through tears that streamed down his face. "I don't like staying at Auntie's. I like being at home with you."

Squeezing his tiny hand, Mom reassured, "I don't have to work every day — just when they call me. So you can still stay home with me most of the time."

"Is that really so?" he questioned.

"Yes, I only have to go when they call me and if Auntie can watch you that day."

"So you don't have to go to work tomorrow?" he questioned again.

"No, I don't. You will be home with me." Mom smiled at her sad, youngest boy.

He stopped, wrapped his body around her legs, hugged her, and repeated, "Thank you, Mommy, thank you, Mommy."

By the time they had walked the few blocks home, he was swinging her hand and telling her what they would do together tomorrow after they had breakfast, and Dad had left for work and the other kids had left for school.

When they arrived home, the whole family gathered to hear about Mom's first day at work.

"I entered through the back entrance and waited at the timekeeper's office until the housekeeping supervisor came for me. She showed me how to punch my time card and where to put it. Then we walked to the elevator and went up to the eighth floor to the maids' room, and she selected a uniform for me to wear. She assigned me a locker, gave me the key, and showed me the dressing area.

"After I had changed into my uniform, we went down a different elevator. This one had an elevator man running it, and he asked what floor we wanted. We got off on the floor where the front entrance is. The inside lobby is so beautiful, better than I dreamed it would be, with marble floors and a gold ceiling with tall arches, taller than anything I have ever seen. The furniture is fit for royalty — the Queen may have even stayed there. I met the manager and the front desk lady and then the supervisor showed me the ballrooms, meeting rooms, and public washrooms. I don't get to clean those areas yet. I have to start with cleaning the guest rooms." She finally took a breath, trying to figure out what to tell us next as we sat captive to her words.

Smiling, she continued, "I saw the guest rooms I would be cleaning. I get my own passkey to the rooms. I tap on the door a few times and call out, 'Housekeeping,' and wait a few moments for someone to answer. If no one answers, then I enter the guest room and begin my work. Every room has its own bathroom with a sink, toilet, tub and shower, and tiled floor. In the bedroom, the floor is marble except for the area where the bed is, which is carpet. And the beds have fancy bedspreads and white sheets and pillowcases. Then the housekeeping supervisor showed me the Vice Regal Suite ... it is huge and plush, ten times bigger than our house. The bedroom has velvet curtains and a king-size four-poster bed fit for the Queen. That is my favourite room! There is a great big living room where you can see the river and the city from huge windows. Besides that, there is a sitting room and two bathrooms. The furniture looks like what you see in fancy magazines about castles."

She sat back for a moment, catching her breath. Then she smiled broadly and said, "The supervisor said I can bring my family to the hotel and show you the inside. Would you like to come and see The Castle?"

With that, there was an uproar of "Oh Mom, really, you can take us inside The Castle?"

Even Dad, who didn't want Mom to return to work, finally relented. He knew how taken Mom was with The Bessborough and her plan to buy a new house and finally he admitted that he, too, would love to go. So began our family connection to The Castle on the River.

The tapping of the key along with the word *Housekeeping* became a trademark of Mom for our family. In later years, when we stayed at The Bessborough, Mom would stop in and check how our stay was. She would tap on the door three times with her key, call out "Housekeeping" and then enter our room — just as she had been taught to do before entering to clean a room when regular guests occupied it.

"Is everything good with the room?" she would ask. She never stayed long, just long enough for a quick hello and a hug before continuing on with her workday.

By 1962, Mom had secured full-time employment at the stately hotel. The air force barracks had closed but Dad had found new employment elsewhere. Now with both of them working full-time, in 1963, they were able to buy the new family home, achieving Mom's dream.

However, within two years after the family move, Dad's arm began to lose mobility and strength and the pain intensified. Mom became the primary financial support for the family, taking on the management of the family finances. Dad became what he called "the chief cook and bottle washer" for the family and was known for his tasty soups and hash. He always said that the sign of a good cook was when you can go into the cupboard and fridge and make something tasty with what little is there. He excelled at this.

Just as the Bessborough Hotel symbolized hope, progress, and prosperity for the citizens of Saskatoon in the mid-1930s, it became the economic anchor and symbol of hope, progress, and prosperity for Mom and our family in the 1960s. Thus, Mom's job at The Bessborough took on a more significant role than she and the family anticipated when she first started working there part-time.

The life of a working mom with a family of eight is difficult and demanding today and was even more so in the 1960s when it was unusual for women to work outside the home. Once Mom started working full-time, the kids had to pitch in at home. Saturday was housecleaning day, whether Mom was away at work or not. Dad was the taskmaster. No one could go out until the house was clean for Mom to come home to.

As Dad became responsible for household activities, Mom took on more planning and administrative roles. One of my favourite memories was of Mom sitting at the kitchen table with her clump of bills, the previous month's tattered calculation sheet, and pencil in hand; she would calculate and recalculate where the money would be spent. We would tease Mom that she was doing her "gazintos" again, just like Jethro from The Beverly Hillbillies when he tried to solve his math problems. With a grimaced smile and a furrowed brow, she would wave her hand, shooing us away from bothering her.

Mom was a decisive and expert planner once she figured out how to fulfill a need. While she was working, time was at a premium, so grocery shopping with her was like entering one of those cross-Canada treks you see athletes do on TV. She had a list, cash, and focus. There was no stopping to check labels. You were in and out and on the way home in record time. Mom's grocery shopping team would have won all the races! It was what I call power shopping — planned and deliberate.

Only after she retired did Mom embrace return and leisure shopping. I noted the change when, for three years in a row, after my careful selection of high-fashion Christmas outfits for her, she returned them. In fact, she returned one three times. The first time, she returned the outfit and exchanged it for one she liked. When she tried it on at home, she no longer wanted it. She then exchanged it for a different outfit. When she tried the newest selection at home, she decided that it didn't suit her, so she once more returned and purchased another. This time, she was satisfied with her selection and proudly wore her new outfit! By the time she completed all the exchanges on this final Christmas outfit, it may well have become her new Easter outfit!

In her later years, her decision-making for day-to-day things, such as what she should eat when we went out for dinner, was painful to witness. Ordering drinks was pretty straightforward and didn't take much thought as we all had our favourites: Caesars for all, or Caesars for Mom and me, and wine for my sisters. My sister Wanda and I would be quick to select from the menu. Meanwhile, Mom and my sister Winnifred would chat back and forth, trying to draw us into their indecision about what food they should order. That was the complexity of Mom's decision-making. Significant matters went on the "I need to pray and ask for guidance" list, and, with guidance, made a decision; yet when it came to the day-to-day, simple decisions in her personal life, like what to order for dinner, she was a ditherer.

Mom worked her financial magic throughout the year to meet household obligations, family needs, and special occasions. Though money was often scarce, her resourcefulness always met our basic needs and more. On our birthdays, we received a small gift. She made her best-ever chocolate cake and decorated it with slightly-used candles, representing the birthday child's age. She tucked coins into birthday cakes before icing them. As kids, we were so excited to receive a piece of cake with a coin. Over time, the coins were wrapped in tin foil. Later, as we all became teenagers, the coins disappeared altogether. Every Christmas, she ensured that each family member received a special gift and that the Christmas season was bountiful with food and drink and time with extended family. Christmas was Mom's favourite time of year.

The work Mom performed cleaning hotel guest rooms was labour intensive. Every room had to be cleaned to a high standard and checked by the assistant housekeeper. It would have to be redone if it was not up to par. However, Mom never had to redo any of her rooms. Instead, she strove for and exceeded expectations. She took immense pride in performing her duties, taking extra care in the Vice Regal Suite, imagining that she and Dad would stay there one day.

Mom's day started with the sudden, piercing ringing of her wind-up alarm clock. She would pop out of bed and begin her morning ritual. She was in high gear every morning. High gear was her natural rhythm. It took her less than fifteen minutes to dress, wash, and comb her hair, put on her favourite red lipstick, and be ready to go to the bus stop.

The part of her morning routine she loved best

was softly waking each of her six children with a kiss on the forehead. Each morning, we would get a "Good morning Sunshine, it is time for you to get up; I am off to work." Sometimes, we would have traces of red lips on our foreheads as we looked in the mirror to brush our hair.

After waking us, if she had time for breakfast, it would be toast and instant coffee, which she consumed while standing near the kitchen window watching for the bus. Her half-empty coffee cup with red lipstick marks and a plate of partially eaten toast would be left on the counter as she rushed out the back door to the bus stop on the corner.

The family dog, Trixie, silently followed Mom during her morning activities. After Mom's workday, the dog knew Mom would be coming home and she would sit on a chair by the window, watching for her to get off the bus. Once Trixie spotted Mom, she would alert the family that Mom was home by barking, dancing in circles, and heading toward the back door. *Yes! Mom was home!* We children felt the same way.

When the family moved to the new house, Dad was still working. If he was working the day shift, he and Mom would ride the bus together, sitting side-by-side and talking and laughing along the way, much like they did when they used to walk to work to the hospital together when they were first married.

Mom and Dad loved that time — their time together united in supporting their family.

Mom would often arrive home from work with pain in her arms and back from constant repetitive motion. Her legs and feet would ache from the many miles she walked and the hours she stood during her workday. Once in the door, she would remove her nylon stockings and wash her feet in the tub. This daily routine of soaking her aching feet and a few minutes of quiet time was a transition from work to home life. Often Dad and I would prepare supper. If not, Mom would prepare it without complaint and then set out to complete daily household tasks until her usual, late-hour bedtime.

As you can imagine, life at home with a family of eight could be chaotic and with Mom working full-time, there was little time for socializing. So, Mom's work in the elegant Castle became her sanctuary and she enjoyed and thrived at her job. She generally had Sundays and Mondays off, which allowed her to regularly attend Sunday mass, which was vital to her.

On her Mondays off, the children would look forward to Mom being home and preparing lunch and supper. She would bake her fluffy, homemade bread and do the family laundry using the wringer washer machine and a rinse tub. When she found time to talk on the phone with her sisters while doing tasks, we would have to duck under the stretched-out phone cord to pass through the hallway. We knew the sisters were sharing confidences when she tucked herself into her bedroom with the telephone cord outstretched and held tight by the closed bedroom door. Sometimes, if she took a few minutes to sit while enjoying her telephone conversations, she would find she could not stand up once the conversation ended, as we had tied her apron strings to the chair. This antic amused Mom, but more so we children who lurked about, waiting for her to attempt to get off the chair, each blaming the other for having tied her there.

When Mom began work at The Bessborough, it was still owned by the Canadian National Railway. As a result, staff received a discount on train travel. Mom and our family took advantage of that benefit. One summer, she took her three youngest children and her sister to visit family in British Columbia. Another time, at Christmas, my brother, Wesley, and I travelled by train to Ontario to visit family and friends. We all found train travel very soothing and relaxing. The clicking and clacking of the train wheels and the cars rocking comforted us. The train's rhythm calmed and refreshed Mom, and she felt relaxed and rested after a train ride.

Mom's work at The Bessborough offered her and

our family other benefits besides train travel and discounts on rooms and services. When we were old enough to take the bus, we would meet Mom after work to help her carry the Lost-and-Found items given to staff when they were not claimed after a certain amount of time. This was an exciting event for us. We never knew what treasures we would get from Lost-and-Found; it could be anything from transistor radios and watches to pyjamas, shoes, soaps, shampoo, and perfume.

When the hotel redecorated or purchased new bedding, staff could buy the old items. Many Bessborough blankets and tablecloths are still in the family and used for covering and storing items. Many of our family's furnishings, such as lamps, mirrors, coffee tables, televisions, dressers, chairs, and sofa beds, were acquired from such sales and were staples in our households as we grew up and started living independently. (In the mid-1980s, Wanda and I purchased settees, which we both still have today. Wanda recently recovered hers, so it could again regally adorn her living room.)

Generally, the four youngest WJKs would meet Mom on Lost-and-Found pick-up day. The little group of us stood at the back door entrance, watched the other workers exit The Bessborough, and waited for Mom to come out and get us. At this particular time, the hotel was renovating, and furniture and bedding were gathered in back hallways for staff to look at and purchase. So, after checking in at the back service desk, away we went with Mom to view and select items for home.

On this particular day, Mom was focused on her list, much like when she went grocery shopping. Her list of items included a television, a coffee table, a lamp, and blankets. As we passed the bedroom furniture that lined the massive back hallway, Mom noted, "These beds and dressers are too big for our tiny bedrooms." Always very respectful in Mom's place of work, we all nodded in agreement and followed her to the television and lamp section. There were a variety of sizes, and after much discussion about what size of television could fit into our small living room, Mom finally decided the mid-sized one was right for us. Next, Mom selected some heavy blue bedspreads. We were so excited — everyone was getting a new Bessborough blanket. A small table lamp and a well-built coffee table that could withstand the weight of many children climbing on it were selected. (Somewhere in the years ahead, that coffee table made its way to my cabin and served us well for many seasons.)

On the way out, Mom told the back service desk man what items she wanted. He would tag them and prepare an invoice for her to settle when she picked them up. We were so pleased about our new Bessborough purchases that we almost forgot the Lost-and-Found bags held at the service desk for Mom.

There were two large bags, and we stopped outside the back door and opened both of them, looking inside with anticipation. We quickly divided the items, using extra paper bags we had brought from home so that we could each carry a bag. On the bus ride, we had plenty of time to check the bags we carried and attempt to claim a particular item as our own. Mom's rule was that no one could make a final pick until she looked at all the items. We could say what we wanted, but Mom was the boss of who got what from the Lost-and-Found treasures.

Mom was like Mrs. Hughes, the Head Housekeeper from Downton Abbey, and her work brought her great satisfaction and pride. She learned many new things, both work- and life-related, while working at The Bessborough; she was a lifelong learner, long before that term was coined. Mom learned all the intricacies of cleaning the entire hotel, from hallways and offices to ballrooms and her favourite, the Vice Regal Suite. She quickly understood the importance of the housekeeping division to the smooth operation of the hotel and how all the departments worked together to provide patrons seamless and high-quality service. She took her part in providing leadership and superior service to heart, performing her duties to ensure The Bessborough presented a sparkling clean and magnificent hotel for its patrons. She was promoted to Assistant Housekeeper for her diligent work and ability to learn and train others; in 1988, due to her hard work and dedication, Mom progressed to the role of Head Housekeeper. A few years later, at the age of sixty-eight, she retired from the Castle.

Parallel to Mom's contribution to The Bessborough was what her work there did for her children. Not only was the hotel a stabilizing and economic force in our mother's life, but it was also an avenue for our parents to teach us the value of learning, education, dedication, and hard work.

Foundations and Family Loss

**Wesley, Winnifred, John, Mary, Wanda,
Wayne, Wanita, Wallace, Corina
Klassen Koczka (in front row)**
Mary and John's 30th Wedding Anniversary
1975

Both Mom and Dad promoted further education. "Unless you want to do the kind of physical labour job I have had to do, you need to go to school and get an education," was Mom's repeated phrase. In the background, Dad would echo her sentiment, adding, "Yes, you need to do your homework." Homework was an essential daily activity that had to be completed before we could go out with friends. When we were old enough to get a job, we were encouraged to save money for university or higher education after high school. With only Mom working, our family could not afford to send any of us to higher educational facilities, so saving for our own further education was vital. All of us children either attended university or trained toward the careers we chose.

As we children became old enough to enter the workforce, Mom encouraged us to work part-time at The Bessborough. Other than my oldest brother, Wallace, who was a Navy cadet and therefore had part-time employment while in high school, the WJKs were trained for the work world through The Bessborough and by Mom. These experiences gave us valuable insight into the kind of work that existed, whether we went to university or not.

"When you are given a job to do, do it to the best you can. Do it right so you can be proud of your work no matter what the work is," she repeatedly told us. After we turned sixteen and were able to work at The Bessborough, Mom would consistently get good reports about what fast, respectful, and hard workers her children were. It made us proud to have Mom and her work colleagues notice that we prided ourselves on a job well done, just like Mom and Dad had taught us. Mom led by example, teaching us that hard work was required to succeed. There was no putting things off until tomorrow. Instead, we were taught to do all we could do and then more. And we learned to complete all tasks with a high level of competence. Though she projected herself as a soft-spoken, shy woman, Mom meant business regarding work and showed us the correct way to complete tasks. Her expectations were high, and we were expected to meet and exceed them, no matter what job we performed. She was patient yet firm in her teaching and mentored us to be our best selves on the job.

My sister Wanda tells of her experience being trained by Mom to make up rooms. She recalls she paid attention as Mom — in her work voice — told her all the tasks she was required to do to clean the room. First and foremost, there was the tapping of the key on the patron's door, three times with the call "Housekeeping," the few moments' wait and then the entrance. My sister said she learned how to undress and dress a bed properly with wrinkle-free sheets and the bedspread folded and tucked. It took her a while to master the technique with speed, and she was so proud when Mom told her she was as fast and good as any of the other housekeepers.

Mom's expectations of excellent hotel service also extended to the hotels she stayed in. Whenever Mom would check into a hotel room, one would find her looking first to see if the bed was made correctly by moving the pillows, pulling back the bedspread, and examining how the sheets were tucked. After that, her well-trained eye would sweep the room to verify cleanliness and that items were placed correctly. The bathroom was scrutinized next, with her looking for a spotless sink and bathtub, ample towels properly folded, and the presence of complimentary personal care items. After that, the closet was examined. Last, she would inspect the curtains and window, scanning the outside area as she opened them. After the room inspection, she was down the hallway, looking for the housekeeping staff to discuss her work and her family and tell them the room was well-appointed and clean.

Mom was proud to share that she also worked at a hotel, at "The Castle on the River." It was as if Mom and other hotels' housekeeping staff were part of a family that the rest of us knew nothing about. Mom taught us to be courteous to the hotel staff, and most importantly, to always leave a tip for the housekeeping staff. To this day, we always leave a tip with a note of thanks.

During her lifetime, Mom experienced both joy and heartbreak. She endured many hardships, especially with the death of her mother in 1973, her husband John in 1980, and her oldest son, Wallace, in 1981.

Mom had a strong bond with her mother, who died of a heart attack when Mom was fifty-seven years old. Mom would say she needed her mother for a lifetime but was grateful she had her as long as she did. Mom's mother was a shy, soft-spoken German woman. She looked like the grandma you would see in children's picture books from days gone by — with round glasses perched on her small nose, a short, very roundish body, and a long, dark-coloured dress with a shawl covering her shoulders. Her long grey hair was always neatly tucked in a bun at the back of her head. I would feel comfort from her whenever she entered the room. I am sure my Mom felt the same way. Grandma was the matriarch of the family even though her husband was the traditional "Let's get this done!" German commander. My mother had a mix of both her parents' characteristics.

In the mid-1960s, Dad had seen a doctor and was told if he didn't change his lifestyle by smoking and drinking less, he would be dead in a few years. I am sure that prediction played over and over in Mom's head and she counted each day with her Johnny as a blessing. For years after that warning, my mother tried to get my father to once again see a doctor, but after all the suffering he had endured with his arm, Dad avoided any sort of further medical intervention.

In 1980, in late spring, Dad began not feeling well. His stomach was swollen, and painful, he could not keep food down; he coughed up a lot of phlegm, and he could hardly smoke. Mom tried to convince him to see a doctor or go to the hospital, but he refused. Finally, one day in late July 1980, he agreed to go to the hospital. In less than a week, Mom's Johnny was gone.

Our father was dead. Though one can anticipate and understand that death is near, when it occurs, it still shakes you to the core, causes heartache, and is final. Dad passed away in the hospital with Mom at his side and our family there supporting both of them.

Mom was despondent for some time, going through the motions, feeling nothing but pain and sorrow. After much prayer, she came to accept that it was the Lord's plan that her husband be taken and that Johnny would suffer no more.

She never re-married. She said that no one could replace Johnny. He was her one and only true love. Mom immersed herself in work and church activities, occupying herself as she learned to accept the loss of her one true love. However, he was ever-present in her heart and mind.

At the time of her husband's death, except for one adult child, Wanda, who was living at home while she attended university, Mom had no child-rearing responsibilities. The youngest, Wayne, was twenty-three years old and living in Calgary. However, my mother firmly believed that a mother never stops mothering; it was a lifelong commitment, an eternal bond of unconditional love. The same unconditional love she committed to and showed her husband. She looked upon the harshness she sometimes felt from my father as preparing her for life without him, so she could manage the disappointments and tragedies that would befall her throughout her life after he was gone. This belief served her well.

Her Bessborough family took on a more significant role in her life. These relationships at work expanded her already accepting attitude. Mom was always open to learning about and accepting differences. Many of the workers at The Bessborough were immigrant women from various countries; they invited her to family gatherings, shared their confidences with her, and looked to her for advice and guidance. She made life-long friends with many of them. When they visited their homelands, they would bring her special gifts in appreciation for her friendship and kindness. Mom was regarded as a wise, kind, genuine, hardworking, progressive woman of faith, with a good sense of humour.

Mom was a fun loving, active, and attractive woman. I remember a call from her several years after Dad's death, telling me about a former neighbour who had asked her to go for coffee with him. Her voice was high pitched and she spoke quickly, "Can you believe it, Raymond asked me to go for coffee with him? Why would I want to go for coffee with him? What could he want from me? I told him I was busy and I hung up." That was her prevailing attitude towards male companionship after Dad's death, although she loved spending time with her father, her brothers, and brothers-in-law.

In November of 1981, at the age of thirty-five, my brother, Wallace, took his own life. Mom said he had always done many crazy deeds, but she had never expected this. His death was a very traumatic, haunting loss for Mom and our family. After a period of shock and disbelief, Mom eventually accepted the loss of her son, but she could never understand the pain he must have felt to choose death over life. He had been a successful man by any measure: he was tall, handsome, charismatic, a District Director for a retail company in Alberta at the time of his death.

Mary and John
30th Wedding Anniversary
1975

Mom would often talk about how great a speaker Wallace was. She was proud he was selected as Valedictorian for his Grade Twelve graduating class and loved his inspiring speech. He was a family favourite and as he grew older, he was often called upon to emcee many family celebrations, like our parents' 30th Wedding Anniversary in April 1975 and our grandparents' 65th Wedding Anniversary.

Mom often said it was difficult to let go of her mom and her husband, but they had lived many years. The most challenging thing she ever had to do was bury her firstborn son, at an early age. The loss of Wallace left a void in Mom's heart that could not be filled — no matter how much she prayed. (Decades later, in March 2013, she would have to bury another son, sixty-three-year-old Wesley, and she echoed the exact phrase, "A mother should never have to bury a child." This death, too, was difficult for Mom to comprehend, but for a different reason; by this time, she was beginning to experience symptoms of dementia.)

Mom's father-in-law and mother-in-law, who were very close to her, died in 1980 and 1981. Her mother-in-law had treated her as a daughter, and though she did not replace Mom's mother, she provided a mother's comfort to Mom. The loss of family icons — her mother-in-law and father-in-law, her husband,

and her firstborn son, in such a short time was heart-crushing for Mom.

However, Mom's work, prayer, and immense faith brought her some peace as she came to accept the finality of death, and life without many significant loved ones. She had special masses said for them, prayed and lit candles for them, visited their graves, and shared fond and funny memories of them with others. She found comfort in knowing they were still with her in spirit and that one day, she would reunite with all her beloved family. She came to accept death, though she didn't like or understand it.

Throughout our lives, Mom and her work at The Bessborough remained a constant. In the 1990s and early 2000s, Mom saved enough money so she could travel — and did so with her daughters Winnifred and Wanda. Some of the places they travelled to were Europe, Mexico, Cuba, and Las Vegas. Our family had spread out from Halifax to Victoria, and she visited us all frequently. Mom spent more time at our homes and the lake once she retired. She enjoyed our family, and we enjoyed sharing our lives with our beloved mother.

Besides being a place of work and a training ground, the Bessborough Hotel was the family event venue of choice. Mom's surprise 65th birthday party was held in the Vice Regal Suite of the Bessborough Hotel. It was humbling, yet the dream of a lifetime come true, for Mom to have a special event in her honour at the Bessborough Hotel and to be able to sleep in the Vice Regal Suite she loved. She was overjoyed and proud to host her family and friends in this exclusive locale she had only once dreamt about.

Although Mom was never able to spend a weekend at The Bessborough with Dad, which they had dreamed of so many years ago, her Johnny was there at the Bessborough Hotel in spirit the weekend of her 65th birthday celebration. She never became a Princess to live at The Bessborough with Johnny, her Prince, but she loved the life she had lived with him.

Wanda had her wedding at The Bessborough. She and her husband are still married; their marital longevity might be due to the magic of their castle-like hotel wedding! It is still the hotel of choice when Wanda and her husband visit Saskatoon. Wesley often stayed at The Bessborough when he came to Saskatoon for work. My husband, Earl, and I spent many anniversaries at the grand hotel, courtesy of Mom, who received an employee discount on guest rooms. There were many special family meals in restaurants at the Castle on the River. Some WJKs participated in its nightlife in the '70s and '80s; and the Blues Festival at The Bessborough Gardens were a staple for Mom and our families during those years. Our family loved music, and the well-treed and manicured Bessborough gardens presented a beautiful setting for bands and music lovers.

When Mom retired from the Bessborough Hotel in 1991 at sixty-eight years of age, a grand party with a family supper was held for her. She was ambivalent about retiring as her work had been a significant part of her life and a stabilizing force for over thirty years, but she trusted her faith and intuition that it was time for her to retire and take on a new adventure and chapter in her life. As always, she embraced the challenge and gracefully accepted the change.

In 2001, at seventy-eight, Mom sold her house and moved to a penthouse suite in a senior's high rise near the Market Mall. In early 2014, the family moved Mom to a personal care home in Prince Albert, where she lived for the remainder of her life. She sometimes regarded it as a hotel — using hotel terms such as lady at the front desk, housekeeping, and houseman. Her more than thirty years of working at The Bessborough profoundly impacted her life and the lives of our family. Her work at the hotel enabled her to support her family and set herself up for a comfortable retirement.

Mom was invited to the Bessborough Hotel's 65th Anniversary in January 2000. She invited her family to attend and her daughter-in-law, who accompanied her, still marvels about that day and how proud Mom was to be invited to participate and be acknowledged for her work, leadership, and positive influence at The Bessborough. What a positive testament to Mom and her reciprocal relationship with the hotel, Mom's "Castle on the River."

Though her job was not glamorous, she loved the hotel and the work. She was proud that five of her six children had worked there and sometimes with her. When my sister, Wanda, worked in housekeeping, Mom taught her how to make a bed properly, a standard she still keeps. I always enjoyed working at The Bessborough. Like my Mom, I thought of it as an elegant castle.

Wesley and I would serve banquets, sometimes working together with our mother. She was always proud to work alongside us. With one exception. We were serving an elite banquet in the Adam Ballroom. I was carrying a tray of twenty-six soups above my shoulder (as the fancy servers do), when my shoulder gave way. The clang of the tray and the sound of breaking glass abruptly interrupted the gallant affair. As the soup slowly spread across the marble floor, all the sound was sucked out of the room, momentarily stopping time. After the moment of silence, life and sound returned to the elegant dining hall, but all eyes were on me. I was so embarrassed, I wanted to run and hide. But Mom and Wesley quickly fetched another tray of soup and helped me serve it safely. Aside from that episode, and the one occasion when while serving a banquet, I dropped a green olive down the back of an evening gown-clad patron, my employment record there is un-spillable.

As I reflect on the Castle on The River, I see it as a foundation for Mom, a stately anchor, esteemed, magnificent, and full of beauty. It was an elegant land, both a refuge and workplace, for Mom to enter daily.

The Bessborough Hotel provided Mom and our family an excellent opportunity to support ourselves and learn about work and life while enjoying the elegant atmosphere. We are grateful to Mom and the Bessborough Hotel for the underpinnings of life she and the castle afforded us.

The Family Move

John, Wallace, Mary (holding Wayne)
Wanita (in front of Wallace), Wesley (in front of Mary), Wanda,
unknown neighbour girl (possibly sister-in law Betty Hersberger)
Winnifred
1958

Working outside the home was a life-changing opportunity for Mom as she found greater independence and enjoyed a sense of pride and accomplishment from her work. Though she felt satisfied with her job, she was motivated by her goal: to save money for a down payment on a new house for the family. The marginal neighbourhood we lived in was not the kind of area she wanted her children to grow up in.

Mom was a planner and purposeful, rarely spontaneous. Life with my father and so many children had taught her that one must manage situations as they arise, but one must also think ahead, anticipate, and plan to get what the family needed. Her intuition was strong. She was tuned into life and generally had a way of knowing something was happening or was about to occur before being told about it. She believed hard work and perseverance were necessary for success in life — that and, of course, prayer.

By 1962, she had secured full-time employment at the Castle on the River and could now execute her plan to buy a new family home. Though she and Dad had discussed purchasing a new home in the future, she had yet to share with Dad that she was already putting money away for a down payment.

In early 1962, Dad received notice that his employment at the Royal Canadian Air Force

Station was being terminated and he would receive a severance payment. Once the station closed, he found full-time work as a janitor. Mom was confident that she could meet the financial obligations of the family once Dad's employment ended even if he could not find a new job quickly. She had carefully calculated the down payment, the cost of a new house, moving expenses, and cash from the sale of the old home. With her savings and Dad's severance, there would be enough money to purchase a new house that would better serve their growing family and her goals for her children's success of life.

This turn of events regarding the severance spurred Mom to more earnestly convince Dad that a move to a new house suitable for the family was necessary — now, while they had a lump sum of cash. Mom's vision was clear. She wanted a safe and nurturing home and community for her family. The new home would have a gas furnace, running water, and an indoor bathroom with a bathtub. It would have a big kitchen and dining area for the family to sit together and eat. It would have separate bedrooms for the boys, the girls, and for her and Dad. It would be large enough that she could invite extended family for special occasions.

The area would be safe to walk after dark, with no groups of kids roaming the streets, looking for trouble. The neighbourhood must be clean and the neighbours invested in caring for their children and keeping them safe. The schools had to have teachers who took an interest in their students, with activities, sports, and opportunities for the children to learn and grow into successful, well-adjusted adults.

In 1963, we were a family of eight — Mom and Dad and six children, the WJKs. The house we lived in on Avenue O South since the mid-1950s was new when Mom and Dad purchased it, but it had no running water or furnace, only a wood stove in the small kitchen and an oil burner stove in the basement to augment the wood heat in the winter. It was a small two-room house sided with the red and black speckled asphalt siding of the day. A white picket fence framed the front yard. Today, the house could be considered a rustic combination of a tiny and off-the-grid house. Perhaps the still rural, yet urban, area captured the farm hearts of Mom and Dad when they purchased it. It was simple and homey.

The house served the family well. It had a huge yard. In the colder months, the backyard was home to a large, lit skating rink. During our long Saskatchewan winters, it is dark by five in the evening, so the lights were essential if us kids wished to use the rink after supper. In the winter, our backyard rink became the hub of the neighbourhood. Kids would bring their skates and hockey sticks, play for a while, and then warm up in our back porch before going out for their last skate before heading home.

In the spring, part of the backyard was transformed into a garden filled with fragrant flowers, healthy vegetables, and massive hills of potatoes. All able-bodied family members participated in maintaining it. There was still enough yard left for play and even though there was a park only a block away, the yard and back alley were used for games of can-can and baseball. The woodshed, coal bin, and the playhouse were great hiding places for the neighbourhood game of hide and seek.

The main floor of the house had only two rooms and a porch. The small kitchen adjacent to the tiny dining/living room held a wood-burning stove. (Today, this would be called an *open concept*.) The kitchen table had fold-out leaves that could only be opened for meals, as the room was so small. Every few days, the sweet smell of fresh bread baking wafted out of the woodstove oven, filling the small yet comfortable house.

Downstairs, through a trap door, were two bedrooms. An oil-burning heater sat at the entrance to the larger of the two rooms. During winter, you could smell a hint of oil from the stove as the flames frolicked behind the round, smoke-covered glass on the door.

There were rules about the use of the trap door that everyone knew and had to obey. For example, the back door could not be left open over the trap door or a person could not climb upstairs from the basement. If a person was downstairs in the basement and heard someone leave the back door open on top of the trap door, they would have to immediately pound on the trap door so the person going out would come back and close the back door properly so the trap door could be pushed open. The trap door also had to remain closed at all times so no one could accidentally tumble down the stairs into the basement.

Over the years, many minor mishaps regarding the trap door occurred. Wesley and I played horsey when we were ages 6 and 5. It was my turn to be the horse, and he was riding on my back. The horse was on its hands and knees with the rider on its back. The horse had to sprint on all fours from one end of the tiny house to the other, quickly turn around while trying to buck the rider off, and then head back across the house to do the same thing at the other end. As I turned around to head back the other way, my finger got caught in the metal ring handle used to pull the door open. I dropped to the floor, and my brother fell off my back onto the floor beside me. He lifted the handle and freed my finger, and blood gushed from it. It was a dramatic event with me jumping up and down, crying and yelling and holding my finger, which had blood-soaked my blouse. My fingernail fell off after the wound healed. The tip of my index finger is still lopsided and scarred because of the incident.

We children slept downstairs, girls on one side of the wall and the boys on the other. On the girls' side, there was a large crib with a cast iron frame — what we would call a *day bed* today. That was the bed for the youngest family member once they got big enough to sleep independently. The upstairs living room doubled as a bedroom for Mom and Dad.

Even though the house was small, it was clean, comfortable and welcoming. It was a gathering place for family and extended family. Grandpas, grandmas, aunts, and uncles would visit and sometimes stay overnight, shuffling kids around to make space for additional people to sleep. Though our family had little money, everyone was welcomed and offered food, drink, and a place to sleep if needed.

While the other mothers in the neighbourhood had bathrooms with running water, our Mom did not. Dad ran a hose from Mr. Vera's, our neighbour, and filled the large metal barrel inside our enclosed, unheated porch. Mom heated water on the wood stove for cooking, cleaning, and bathing. There were four different washing vessels: a large porcelain dishpan for dishes only, a smaller porcelain pan for hand washing, a huge metal aluminum tub for bathing, and a small baby-only enamel bathtub that could sit on the washstand. On laundry day, Mom would put a massive copper boiler wash tub used to heat water for washing clothes, on the stove and fill it with water from the barrel. Although a hot water reservoir was built into the stove, it did not hold enough water for washing clothes. In the warm months, the rinse tub (which doubled as our bathtub) and the washer would be used in the closed-in porch where they were stored. In cold months, Mom dragged the washer, rinse tub, and a chair to set the rinse tub on, into the kitchen.

There was no room to move around in the house once laundry day was in motion. Mom sorted the dirty laundry of our family of eight by colour and arranged the clothes into piles around the kitchen and tiny living room. If you messed with her piles, you would get scolded. Whites always came first, and dark clothing last.

Mom would brave the elements in both summer and winter to hang the clothes on the line outside. In the winter, she would wear her winter coat and gloves to hang the clothes and retrieve them. When she brought them in, the clothes would stand up on their own. Then, she would wrestle with the frozen items of clothing to get them onto the dryer rack, which was placed in the porch or the kitchen, depending on the time of year. I still recall the scent of fresh, frozen clothes thawing by the warmth of the kitchen wood stove.

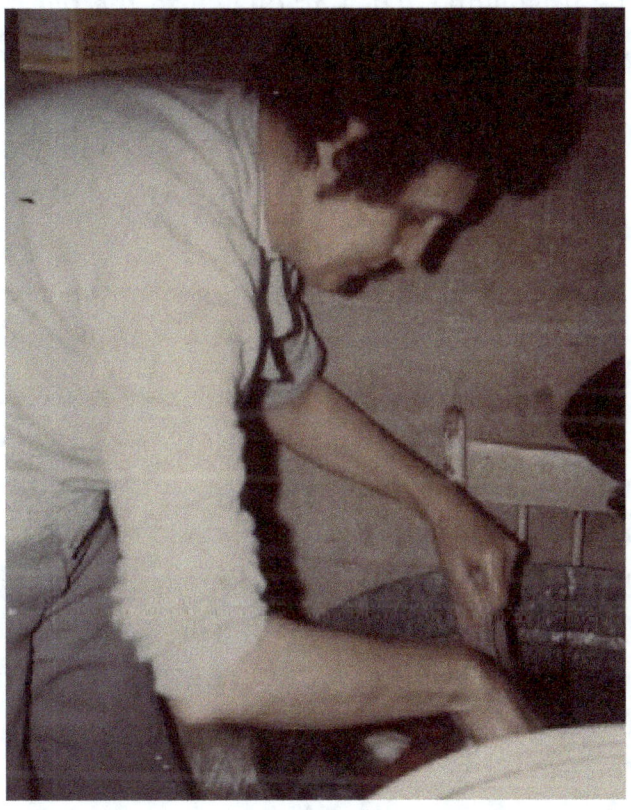

Mary
washing clothes in the house on Avenue O
early 1960s

Bathing was a major production, with the huge copper boiler being called for duty again. As with clothes washing, there was a process. In the warm months, bathing occurred in the porch with a blanket hung for privacy. Mom, the bath master, could come and go as required and would supervise and assist the bather. Babies were daily sponge-bathed or bathed in a porcelain pan in the kitchen on the washstand. They graduated to the big metal tub once they grew too big for the baby wash pan.

The weekly baths started with the smallest always getting fresh, warm water. Mom would wash the little ones with a washcloth, soaping them up and washing their hair.

Hair was rinsed with warm vinegar water while you held a face cloth over your eyes. You then stood up, and Mom wrapped you in a towel and dried you off. Clean pyjamas were mandatory and felt good. Another WJK, this time Wanda, went into the tub with additional warm water. The older kids would wash themselves, but Mom always poured the warm vinegar water over our heads to rinse our hair. And so it went until all the WJKs were clean, and poor Mom was exhausted.

The bathing process is a vivid, fond memory for me:

"*Wanita, come in. It's time for your bath,*" *Mom calls out to the yard as the sun begins going down.*

"A few more minutes, Mom, I want to play with the big kids," I yell back.

It is summer, Saturday night, and bath night. I can hear Hungarian dance music playing from Mr. Vera's next door. He must have company again. People are singing. I can hear my Dad harmonizing.

"Get in here. It's your turn," she calls again.

I stop in the outhouse before heading for the house. I pass by the tub in the porch, slip into the kitchen and get a drink of water before my bath. The three youngest WJKs are sitting in a row on the couch, with my youngest brother in the middle. Winnifred is reading a story to the other two, but not without being corrected as she reads by Wanda, who is younger but knows this story by heart. They have been through the bath.

I return to the porch and undress. The boys know to only come in once their name is called for a bath. With Dad next door at Mr. Vera's house and the young ones on the couch, it's just me and Mom. She brings me a pot of warm water. It's nice to have warm bath water even though I'm the fourth person. I am old enough to wash myself and call Mom when my hair needs rinsing.

She appears wearing her floral apron with big pockets that hold all the little treasures left around the house. If you ask if she has seen this or that, *she magically pulls the item out of one of those big pockets. Her apron is wet, and so is her thick black hair. Her black curls look like they have been fighting with one another, a sign that she has had a busy, tiring day. She has a clean bath towel over her shoulder. She sets down the container of vinegar water, wrings out the family washcloth and places it over my eyes.*

"Hold it tight so the vinegar does not sting your eyes," the bath master instructs me.

"Yes, Mom, ready," I reply as she begins to pour warm vinegar water over my head.

"Tip your head back," she coaches.

And I do. I can feel Mom's fingers gently rubbing my head as the rinse is poured. I can feel my hair softening as she massages the homemade rinse through my hair. It feels good. Rinse completed, I rub my face with the washcloth and stand for her to wrap me in the clean towel.

I get wrapped in the towel with a hug.

"Thanks, Mom," I say.

She smiles, tells me to get dressed and shouts out the door for Wesley.

I became the keeper of the family metal bathtub, which we still have at the lake. It continues to be used much like Mom used it, to bathe little ones in the kitchen. My kids, nieces and nephews, and grandchildren can all recall bathing in the family metal bathtub in the lake kitchen.

Besides our weekly baths and sponge baths as required, Mom and Dad required daily cleanliness routines for the family. Everyone's before-bed ritual included combing their hair, brushing their teeth, and washing their face and feet. Cleanliness was a team effort, with Dad replenishing the water and Mom and the kids using it.

The last Christmas for our family in the Avenue O South house, in 1962, stands out as an exceptionally happy time. For Mom, who loved Christmas, it was the *Best Christmas Ever!* Everyone was healthy. The tiny house was decked out with Christmas decorations inside and out. A full-sized tree stood before the front door — an entrance rarely used during winter. Dad checked that all the lights were working before setting them on the tree. I was his helper for that, and the entire family participated in decorating with homemade decorations and a few newly purchased sparkling glass balls.

At this time, Dad was working at Royal Canadian Air Force Station and we kids were excited to attend the Children's Christmas party at his workplace. There were games, treats, singing, and a visit from Santa. We all received a gift and a Christmas sock filled with goodies.

Mom and the three oldest WJKs walked to and from midnight mass on Christmas Eve. The three youngest children stayed home with Dad. After the brisk walk home, there was steaming hot chocolate and shortbread cookies and then off to bed so Santa could come. Of course, there were gifts on Christmas morning, many of them! Mom and Dad were both working full-time, so they splurged on Christmas gifts for the kids and for each other. Later in the day, a full Christmas meal was shared with Mom's parents and her youngest brother in our tiny house. This Christmas was embedded in Mom's memory, and she often shared that it was her best Christmas ever. (That is, until her *Christmas-Miracle Christmas*.)

So in early 1963, with years of wonderful memories of the house on Avenue O South still fresh in her mind and the severance payment that came with Dad's recent job loss now available, Mom saw this was the ideal time to purchase the new house they had discussed. Dad was not supportive of purchasing a new house at that time, but Mom's intuition told her that the opportunity might not happen at all if she did not make it happen now. So, with this sense of urgency, Mom laid out her plan to Dad. She got out her pages of calculations and showed him the numbers: her savings, his severance, the sale of the house, the sale of the vacant piece of land that they had purchased earlier. Dad was unaware that she had been saving money for the past three years for a down payment. She made her plea, stating that it was doable even if he didn't maintain full employment.

As she expected, the first few conversations were significant arguments. Dad was furious that she had been saving money without telling him and more upset that she wanted to move now. Several years before, he had bought a piece of property close to the area where she wanted to live and was planning to build a house for the family once they had enough money. But Mom had a bit of a stubborn streak and Dad finally, and reluctantly, gave in to her plan.

This may have been the point where Dad felt the power in their relationship shifting, and that loss of control might have been reason enough to resist. On top of that, he preferred the familiar these days and change was more challenging for him to accept. He had had enough disruption in his life's dreams. Besides, he had friends in the neighbourhood, as did the kids, and he preferred to remain where they were.

Although he agreed to go with Mom to look at potential houses, every house they looked at seemed to have too many negatives for him. Mom was becoming frustrated, but she remained resolute in her quest to buy a house and move the family to a better neighbourhood.

Then, they looked at a house on Avenue T North. The area had a mixture of new and older homes. The neighbourhood looked like the owners took pride in their properties as the houses were in good condition with well-groomed yards and flower and vegetable gardens. The area had wide, paved streets and concrete sidewalks, all in good repair.

The house had red asphalt siding with white trim and a window in every room. There was a wooden step, a landing to the front porch, and a door into the living room. To view the house, they entered from the back door onto a landing that had two steps up to the main floor. Another set of stairs off the landing led down to the basement. From the back door, Mom could see the kitchen and the living room. She was drawn to the enormous kitchen with a dining area on one side. As well as the kitchen and living room, there were also two tiny bedrooms and a large bathroom. Downstairs was a gas furnace, a laundry/storage area, and a large bedroom.

The lot was as big as their yard on Avenue O South, with mature trees and shrubs and a lilac bush. There was plenty of space for a skating rink and a garden. It was close to a park and a playground with a paddling pool. There were two elementary schools a block away. The high school that Wallace attended was only three blocks away.

There was a bus stop on the corner. It would be very convenient for the family.

After much pleading, Mom convinced Dad that *this house* and *this area* were perfect for their family. He finally agreed. They bought the house, and with reluctance, Dad arranged for friends to assist them with moving day. The family would be moved in before the new school year started.

After the house deal was settled and before the family moved in, Mom took all of us kids to view our new home. There were smiles of pleasure on all our faces but ear-to-ear on the faces of the youngest three WJKs as they danced, jumped, and hugged each other as we approached the house. When they got inside, they began to talk nonstop, over one another, about everything this house offered for them and the family. They explored every room several times, bumping into one another as they scooted from room to room. Upstairs, downstairs, and up and down again, planning as they went. Then, they skipped, hopped, and ran around the yard, telling Mom it was big enough to play ball and that the neighbours had kids their age.

My older brothers and I were equally impressed by the new house. It would be great for all of us — close to school, in a nice neighbourhood. Excellent, great idea, Mom! I was sold on it when I saw the indoor bathroom with a bathtub, toilet, and sink. The children's exuberant reaction confirmed for Mom that she had done the right thing for the family in convincing Dad to purchase this new home.

The whole family became focused on the exciting move, Dad a little less enthusiastically. We happily planned and dreamed out loud what life would be like in the new house. We were thrilled to have a bedroom for the boys and a bedroom for the girls, even if we had to share. The boys would sleep in the big bedroom downstairs and the girls in the smaller bedroom upstairs. Each kids' room would have a set of bunk beds and a single bed. All the rooms were larger than in the old house and Mom and Dad would have their own small bedroom, off the kitchen. Our old kitchen table could be left fully open in this kitchen. There was plenty of room for everyone to sit around it. There was space for everyone and everything.

Near the end of summer, our family moved. Moving day could be chaos with six children, however, Mom was focused on moving her family to a better place and she managed the move efficiently with her goal in mind. The three youngest WJKs were left with an aunt for part of moving day. The three oldest WJKs helped with the packing, moving, and unpacking.

The younger three were brought to the new home once the large items and most of the boxes had already been moved. They were even more excited than they were on the day they first visited the new home. In spite of the fact that nothing was in its rightful place and boxes were everywhere, they were overcome with the excitement of moving into their new house. Finally, finally, they could actually sleep in the new house — tonight! When the boxes with their toys and clothes were found, they set about helping one another set up their spaces in their rooms. They were overjoyed to put their own things away. They talked, laughed, and planned what to do in this new house.

Winnifred and Wanda were nine and eight, less than eleven months apart. They were best friends and loved school. Wanda was quite excited about making new friends, while Winnifred expressed her anxiety about school and meeting new people. Wayne, our baby brother, was entering Grade One and would be attending the same school as Winnifred and Wanda. He was a worry-wart and was also anxious about attending a new school. After listening to his tearful fears, both sisters comforted him and told him not to worry; he could walk to school with them, even though the school was only a block away and you could see it from the front yard. They assured him they would check on him at recess and play with him. They consoled him, telling him he would make friends and do well in school, just like them. That satisfied him, so he happily returned to putting his treasures in place.

Later that evening, with a bustle of activity in the house, I entered the bathroom to find my two sisters in the bathtub, one at either end. They were so pleased to have indoor plumbing and a bathtub, they decided to have a bath. They told me the water was very cold. I tried the hot water tap, and they were right; there was no hot water. I reported that to Dad, who checked and discovered that the hot water heater had not been turned on. I boiled several kettles of water and poured them into the bath for my sisters, who had not left the tub in spite of the cold water temperature; they refused to have cold water dampen their first bath experience in the new house.

Over the next week, Mom, Dad, some of their friends, and the three oldest WJKs cleaned, put furniture in place, and unpacked. We also cleaned the old house to get it ready for sale. Wallace, now sixteen, was excited about the new house and that he had helped Mom convince Dad of the benefits of the move. His high school was only a few blocks away, so he would no longer have a long bus ride; he could just walk with his friends. All the rest of us kids would be going to the elementary school one black away.

Wesley and I were a little more than a year apart and typically hung out with our friends or just each other. Although we didn't have any friends in this new area and were both apprehensive about the move, we were looking forward to starting school and figuring out what life would be like in this new house and neighbourhood. Because of our close ages, we would be going into the same grade together. Kids in the new school might think we were twins and I thought that would be amusing. Regardless of our concerns, we were relieved to move to a better neighbourhood; the old one was run down and getting scary after dark.

Dad was taking longer to adapt to the new house and area and often visited his friends in the old neighbourhood. Even Trixie, our dog, who had accepted the new location, went walking with Dad when he visited our old neighbourhood.

By late September, our family had settled into the new house and a new routine. One evening, Mom was sitting quietly by herself at the table in her new kitchen. She had not had a moment of quiet by herself since before the move. While sipping coffee with her monthly budget papers spread on the table, she prayed quietly, expressing gratitude that Dad finally agreed to move and that the children were happy, accepted, and had adapted well to the new house, school, and area. She sighed with satisfaction. They now lived in this house with a big kitchen in a safe and clean neighbourhood. She had met the neighbours; the ones beside them and across the alley were friendly and family-oriented and had kids of similar ages to hers.

Mom reflected on how prayer, diligence, and perseverance had brought the family this far. She thanked the Lord for giving her what she had prayed for. She hoped this house and new neighbourhood would open doors and life chances for her children. She was confident this move would benefit her family as the children grew.

And Mom was right.

After Dad's employment with the Royal Canadian Air Force Station ended, he found full-time employment for a short time. However, due to recurring issues with his injured arm, he eventually permanently stayed home. He received a monthly disability cheque and looked after as much of the household duties as he could.

Mom became mainly responsible for the family's

finances. Her timing to purchase the new house was perfect; it would have been nearly impossible to have saved enough money for the down payment without Dad's severance payment and both of them working for those three years. Though Mom took on the family's financial responsibilities, she still maintained many household tasks that Dad or the children could not do, all the while mothering her children and caring for Dad without complaint.

Though no more children were born to Mom and Dad, the house at Avenue T North was the site of many birthday celebrations. The traditional Christmas and Easter celebrations grew larger with family and extended family and warmed the hearts of all those who joined in, especially Mom's. The Avenue T North home became increasingly like that of my Grandmother's, with a continuous flow of family and friends gracing the household and enjoying Mom's signature chocolate cake and cabbage rolls — always served with genuine hospitality and a smile. Dad would get his fiddle out and tune it repeatedly, "Give me an A.... give me an E...." and so on until it was the right pitch, and finally, music filled the house. Sometimes, other relatives would bring their accordions and guitars, and someone would play the spoons. It was a full-band kitchen party accompanied by singing and dancing. My mother's house was transformed, and so was our mother. She smiled, laughed, and hummed along to the music, enjoying the time with her family. She always looked forward to and cherished family times. Though it was hard to match her genuine kind-heartedness and hospitality, all her children appreciate the family experience of music, dance, and togetherness.

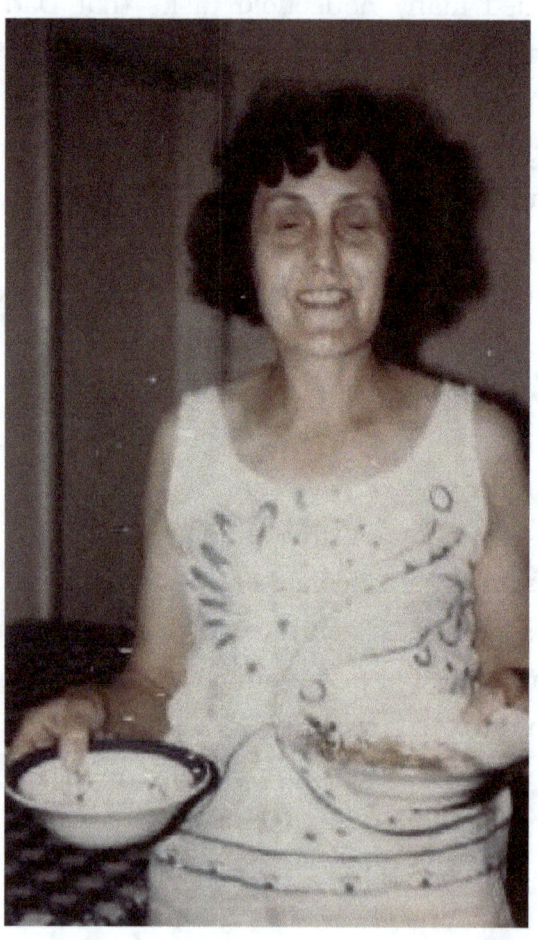

Mary
early 1970s

Mom knew there would be many opportunities for her children in the new area. With the exception of myself, the remaining WJKs all participated and excelled in individual and team sports at school and in the community — with Wayne becoming a personal trainer and Wanda still running half-marathons at sixty-eight.

With encouragement from Mom and Dad, all six WJKs graduated from high school, with four attending university, two obtaining bachelor's degrees, one a doctoral degree in Education, and the other two children attending other higher educational facilities. All went on to successful careers.

Our life chances would have looked different if we had not moved out of that rough neighbourhood. One of my brothers believes that we moved at just the right time; given his group of companions at the time, he may have ended up on the wrong side of the law. (None of us ever ended up in jail — except me, when I pursued a career in the corrections field.) For the younger three WJKs, the move meant feelings of safety and security in a modern home and new beginnings.

As adults, all the WJKs avow that the best thing Mom did for us was to initiate the move from the old neighbourhood to the new one, where we would have more and better opportunities as we grew up. We praised our mother for acting on her intuition and taking the initiative to make a move. Each of us had told Mom this move was a positive, life-changing opportunity for our family.

Mom was a humble woman who did not expect or accept praise well. However, in her mid-life, after repeatedly hearing the positive comments from us, her children, on the family move to Avenue T North, she finally became comfortable with taking the credit she deserved. She acknowledged "the family move" as one of the best decisions she made for our family.

It is funny how the Avenue T North neighbourhood was so safe and inviting for us as kids. When Mom moved from the area in 2001, it was becoming a marginal neighbourhood. Had we all been younger and at home, she would have no doubt taken the initiative to move the entire family to a safer neighbourhood once more.

Vexed Vision

Mary, Winnifred, Ron, Helene Tarko
wedding of Winnifred and Ron Tarko
1998

COURAGE AND A CASTLE

My sister Winnifred remarried in 1998. She and her partner, Ron, had lived together for a few years and decided August was an excellent month for a wedding. She selected the 21st as the date because, for her, the number meant two become one; therefore, the date chosen was August 21. The ceremony would be held in their backyard, with Ron's two children — a married daughter who was seven months pregnant and his son and his partner — attending. Other than the officiant, the only other guests for the ceremony would be the couple's mothers, Mom and Mrs. T. The mothers would be "bridesmothers," as my sister called them, and also act as ring bearers. My sister and her fiancé were overjoyed that their mothers agreed to this special designation in their intimate exchange of vows. After the ceremony, a dinner and dance with forty-four close friends and family members would be held at the Willows Golf and Country Club in Saskatoon.

Friends and family, including the mothers, attended a garden party with a BBQ at the couple's house the evening before the wedding. Both mothers were women of faith; it was common for them to bring out their rosaries, compare them, and discuss the positive attributes of praying the Rosary. Laughter and teasing could be heard when they were together. This evening, the two of them sat across from one another at the kitchen table, playing cards and sharing life stories, having a celebratory drink while the other guests and the prospective bride and groom were in and out of the backyard. Conversations about their children, their deceased husbands, how complex life was now compared to when they were kids, and their favourite foods could be heard by those entering the area. However, the chatter always circled back to the wedding and how nervous they were to be the "bridesmothers" bearing the wedding rings. At some point, my sister heard the musings and decided to alleviate their fear of the rings falling through the slats in the deck. She would pin them to their slips! When she mentioned the plan to the mothers, they both smiled and sighed with relief. They lifted their glasses as if to toast to a great idea.

The wedding day was a warm, bright-blue sky day in Saskatchewan with only a gentle breeze. Before the afternoon ceremony, Winnifred dropped Mom off downtown to have her hair done. A few hours later, she met Mom at the Army and Navy store, located in the building which once housed the iconic Eaton's store.

She smiled as she met Mom at the store's front door. Mom was dressed in her summer pedal pushers, as she called them, with a floral button-up blouse. She had her off-white summer purse tucked tightly between her upper left arm and her upper body with her forearm crossed over her body just above her waist. Mom typically carried her purse this way and did not use the handle; if one wanted to grab her purse and run, well, that would be impossible.

Even though Mom had slept over at Winnifred's house and had been dropped off only a few hours ago, mother and daughter hugged and kissed each other on the cheek as was their usual greeting ritual. Then they started on the main floor, going from aisle to aisle, looking for the items they needed. As they walked, my sister noticed Mom had her glasses in her hand.

"Mum, why aren't you wearing your glasses?" she asked.

"When I walk and look through them, everything looks funny," Mom replied.

"What do you mean 'funny,' Mum?" she asked.

"Depends on where I look," replied Mom. "Like things are sliding and kind of tilted, and the floor feels uneven."

"Are you feeling okay, Mum? Are you sick?" Winnifred questioned.

"I feel fine; we have to hurry," replied Mom, once again the purposeful shopper.

And off they went around the corner and down the stairs to the lower level. My sister watched as Mom held her glasses in her left hand and held onto the handrail with her right. Her purse remained safely tucked under her left arm. Slowly and carefully, one foot was placed on the step, and then the other was placed beside the first. Then the process was repeated for the next step. At this point, my sister held Mom's arm and helped her navigate the steps, continuing to question how Mom felt and what she saw.

Undaunted by the challenge of navigating without her glasses, Mom reassured her she was fine and focused on finding the items for which she was shopping. After she and Winnifred found the desired articles, they decided it was too difficult for Mom to climb the stairs, so they took the elevator to the main floor. The elevator ride with the lady operator, who used a white-gloved hand to open the collapsable side gate before opening the door itself, was always a treat, no matter how many times they rode the elevator. It was particularly welcomed this day as Mom was still experiencing intermittent problems with her world looking sloped, slanted, and wonky. Mom kept putting her glasses on and then taking them off, mostly leaving them off. Noticing this behaviour, Winnifred asked her mother if she needed to have her glasses checked. Mom said they could do that another day; today was the wedding.

Upon further questioning, Winnifred learned

that Mom felt her balance was a bit off as well and that whatever she looked at seemed to be shifting, moving fluidly, or slanted. The situation perplexed both of them.

Ron picked them up at the designated time, and on their way to do a few other errands, they told him about the strange vision Mom had experienced while shopping. They all wondered what was happening to Mom. As they drove, Mom put her glasses back on and reported they were working now and that she could see clearly. However, that improvement was short-lived.

Winnifred helped Mom and Mrs. T dress, fix their hair and makeup, and then readied herself for the ceremony. They all looked beautiful. Winnifred looked stunning in her long flowing gown, a soft green sage with silver flecks glistening in the light. Her necklace with a center pearl feature and her gold earrings complemented her light brunette hair, which was in an updo with curls that cascaded daintily on each side of her coiffed head. Mom wore a peach, calf-length, three-quarter sleeved, belted dress. Her freshly styled ear-length black hair showed a tinge of red. She looked fit to be a "bride's mother." Mrs. T. wore a dark-navy, fitted suit jacket with matching skirt and a crisp, white collared blouse. And like Mrs. T, Mom had one of the wedding rings pinned to her slip so she did not lose it during the ceremony.

Once dressed, both mothers sat in the kitchen and had tea before the wedding. They sipped and giggled like school girls as they showed each other the rings pinned to their slips.

Winnifred sashayed into the kitchen and suggested that the mothers remove the rings so they were not accidentally misplaced while photos of the wedding party were being taken. Both mothers obediently stood as she unpinned the rings and took them to her bedroom for safekeeping.

As she unpinned the ring from her mother's slip, Winnifred noticed her mother's glasses on the table and asked how she was feeling. Mom confirmed that she was still having difficulty with her glasses, and her view was sloped and things looked off kilter when she put them on. But she quickly said she was feeling fine. For pictures, Mom left her glasses on long enough for some photos to be taken and then carried them in her hand.

Once the wedding party returned from taking the pictures, the ceremony in the backyard took place. The service was heartwarming, with both mothers dabbing their eyes with tissues, as they attempted to dry the tears that flowed as their adult children lovingly repeated their vows. When it came to exchanging the rings, both mothers proudly lifted their skirts, showed their slips and the pinned-on rings and offered them to the bride and groom. Now it was time for a toast to the bride and groom and then off to the wedding dinner and dance.

Once they arrived at the Willows, the couple seated their mothers beside one another at the head table and took their seats for the delicious dinner about to be served. After dinner, there were speeches from both the bride and groom, and of course, both mothers said a few words about their role at the ceremony and the rings pinned to their slips, which brought howls of laughter from the crowd.

Winnifred continued to check on Mom and her vision throughout the event. She saw that Mom continued to take her glasses off during dinner and throughout the evening. Each time Winnifred asked her about it, she said that she was having intermittent issues with her glasses, but she was having a wonderful time and felt good. That evening, Mom did not mention her vision issue to anyone but Winnifred and Mrs. T.

Everyone enjoyed the meal, the dance, and each other's company. But the highlight of the evening was the special personal thanks and acknowledgement each guest in attendance received from the bride and groom. The wedding patrons listened attentively as the bride and groom thanked each guest by name for their relationship's unique quality and significance. Sometimes, there was laughter; other times, there was tears. It was a beautiful personal touch of inclusion. From Mom, my sister said she learned inclusion, acceptance, and to celebrate one's gifts.

It wasn't until a month later, when Mom went for a routine medical check-up, that she found out that she had had a stroke on my sister's wedding day. She was very fortunate to have no other medical complications from it, only that her balance was a bit off, and her vision was tilted, off and on, during the wedding day. When Mom spoke of Winnifred's wedding, she rarely mentioned the stroke, she only shared that it was a wonderful wedding and how special she felt being her daughter's "bridesmother," bearing a wedding ring.

My sister and her husband said they felt honoured to have both mothers play such a beautiful part in their wedding and treasure the memories. Winnifred and Mom were both thankful that Mom had only tilted vision on her wedding day, and no lingering effect.

Birthday Slippers

Winnifred and Mary
Mary's 80th Birthday at the spa in Moose Jaw
2004

We have had many memorable birthdays with Mom, but one of my favourites is her 80th birthday celebration. Mom didn't want a big party, so my sisters and I decided to take her away for a weekend to the Temple Gardens Mineral Spa. We agreed to meet in Moose Jaw with Wanda travelling from Weyburn and Winnifred and I bringing Mom from Saskatoon.

The three of us had a laugh-filled travel experience, as Mom was as excited as a young girl going on a first date. She was singing along to music, telling stories about her youth, and telling us Dad would have liked to come to Moose Jaw. She reminded us that one of Dad's standard lines when he disagreed with someone was, "Well then, you go to hell, and I'll go to Moose Jaw." Over the years, we had tried to figure out how he came to have that particular phrase as a comeback, but we could not determine the source. But it always amused Mom and the family.

We had arranged an early check-in, and Wanda was waiting for us in the lobby. We had booked a room with two queen-sized beds. After we unpacked, we headed to our massage appointments at a high-end spa.

The trip to the spa was the weekend's highlight, not because of the exceptional massages but because of Mom's antics with the glittery, black-and-silver, open-toed slippers they gave us to wear when we entered the spa.

The inside of the spa had an Asian décor with beautiful bamboo floors. We were greeted by a friendly staff member who welcomed us warmly as we entered. She asked us to remove our shoes and don the fancy open-toed slippers. There were three generic sizes: small, medium, and large. My sisters and I quickly found slippers that matched our foot size.

Meanwhile, Mom tried on the small ones, walked a bit, and found her foot was too big for the slipper. She tossed that pair aside, selected a medium size, and flip-flopped around the room.

"These are a bit better," she said, her voice filled with determination.

Mom could get her feet all the way in the slipper. But not yet satisfied with the fit, she tried on a larger pair. Even though it was immediately evident that the slippers were too large for her feet, she stood and walked about the room. But with each step, the slippers would come off, and she would have to stop and put them back on. Finally, she just began shuffling, but by the time she got to the other side of the room, her toes and half her foot were entirely outside the front of the slippers. This brought howls of laughter from my sisters and me.

"What's so funny?" Mom asked, perplexed about our laughter; she had been concentrating on making the shoes work.

Disheartened again, she returned to the bench, sat down with a huff and a sigh, threw those slippers into the pile, and selected another medium-sized pair. Her entire foot fit on the platform, and she stood up and started walking around the room once again. But she only shuffled — she did not even try to lift her feet this time. When she returned from her slow walk around the room, only her toes stuck out of the open toe of the slippers. Satisfied that this pair would work, she remarked, "These will be fine."

My sisters and I said in unison, "Mom, those slippers are just fine." By this time, my sisters and I were holding our aching stomachs, laughing at Mom's unusual performance.

The spa attendant returned, having missed Mom's performance trying on the slippers. She led us to another area where we were given tea while we waited for our massages. Mom shuffled to the seating area and sat with her feet firmly on the floor, toes sticking out the end of her slippers, sipping her tea. My sisters and I remained fully amused.

Wanda and I were in the same room for our massages. I selected a hot stone massage as I liked the heat. The massage was excellent and I enjoyed the release of stress from my body; however, the stones were scorching, and I came out with a few red spots on my back. My sister and I spoke very little during our massage, both enjoying the relaxing effects.

Meanwhile, Mom and Winnifred had an adventure in their massage session. They talked and laughed like two schoolgirls on a sleepover. At the end of their treatments, their heads were massaged. When my sister Winnifred and Mom looked over at one another as they got off their beds, they were highly amused and burst into laughter at the sight of their hair sticking straight up as if a lightning bolt had hit them. My sister said they both looked like the singer Billy Idol, a frightful and unbecoming look for both of them.

With the massage adventure behind us and after a stop at the hotel to comb our hair, we went to Hopkins Dining Parlour for dinner. This was not just any dining experience but a refined one in Moose Jaw, a city known for its historic charm.

As usual, Wanda and I quickly selected our meals from the menu ready for the return of the waitress. Mom and Winnifred were still chatting back and forth about what each of them might like. I had almost finished my drink by the time they finally decided on their selections and we could all order our meals. We talked about our massages and laughed about Mom and the slippers. Mom insisted the medium pair was also too big for her, and that's why her toes stuck out. Whatever the reason, it was sure fun to watch. Dinner was delightful, and Mom was in great spirits as she spent the day with all her daughters.

Wanita, Winnifred, Mary, Wanda
celebrating Mary's 80th Birthday in Moose Jaw
2004

Mom was always active, with a healthy, fast pace that many could not keep up with. She wanted to see and do all she could when she was on an outing. This weekend was no different, so after dinner and a quick stop in our room to get our playing money, we were off to the casino. As usual, Mom won some money and my sisters and I barely broke even. But the fun of the casino was watching Mom and feeling her excitement when she won, even just a little, and witnessed the machines flashing and making a triumphant noise.

When we returned to our hotel after a full day of activity, Mom was happy to relax and visit before bed. We reminisced and offered a belated birthday toast to celebrate our incredible day with our beloved mom. We talked and laughed as we lay in bed, saying "Good night, John Boy," as they did on the television show, *The Waltons*, and laughing when Mom or the next sister repeated the same phrase. It took us forever to stop talking and finally go to sleep — where we smiled in our dreams, as we remembered the birthday slippers.

Turbulent Times

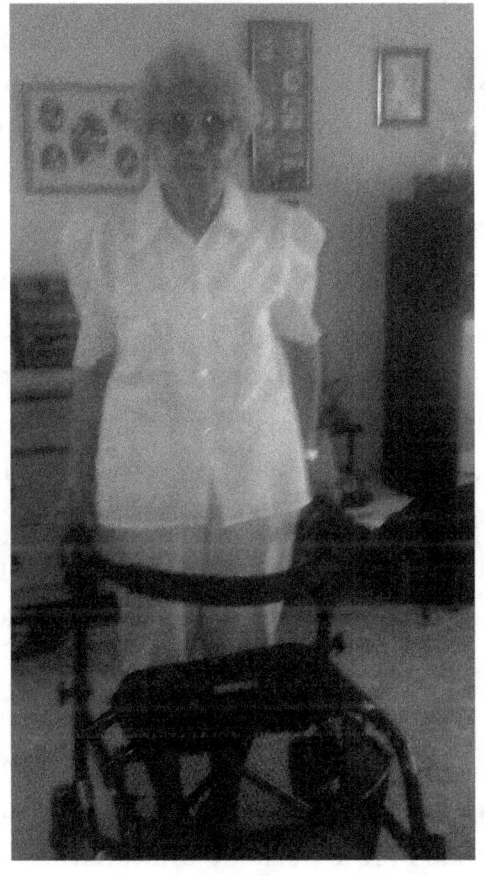

Mary
with her "Queen-like" walker
September 2012

COURAGE AND A CASTLE

At ninety years old, Mom was a healthy, independent, and active woman. She had been living in the seniors' apartment building near Market Mall for twelve years, having moved there from the house on Avenue T North where she had lived for almost forty years and where she and Dad had raised six children. After Dad died in 1980, Mom continued living alone in the house for more than twenty years, looking after the yard, garden, and house — with some help from her children — until she was seventy-eight years old.

Her family called her apartment "the penthouse," as it was on the topmost floor in the senior-only building. Her two-bedroom corner apartment was bright and spacious, with many windows and a balcony overlooking the park and the ball field. From her balcony, she could see the trees in the park and smell the freshness of the outdoors. Across the street was a mall with all the shops she needed for daily living.

There were several seniors' homes with chapels open to the public within walking distance where she could go to mass. One care home had a chapel with a weekly mass on a weekday and another, St. Ann's care home, had masses from Tuesday to Sunday. Generally, Mom attended the Sunday mass at the St. Ann's care home chapel and another mass on a weekday at a different chapel. Mom was active, fit, and walked to and from the services, only taking a cab in the winter when it was too cold to walk.

Two of her sisters lived in a seniors' complex near her apartment building; another sister and her husband lived in their own home nearby. The four sisters spent much of their time together, with a fifth sister who lived in the city occasionally joining in. One of Mom's brothers-in-law fondly called them the "twisted sisters"; when the four of them were together, the stories had so many twists that one never knew what to expect next in the conversation.

Mom was the second oldest of eleven children. Her older sister, Madeline, fondly called the "Queen" by the family, lived in the complex beside Mom's. She usually dressed in high fashion. Though she was of shorter than average height, her presence was immense. The Queen would tell you how she liked things and also what you should like.

The Queen's husband had died more than 20 years earlier and since then, she and Mom had spent as much time as possible together. Mom often walked to the Queen's place, where all the sisters generally gathered. The Queen had difficulty walking long distances, so people came to her. Ergo ... the Queen.

The sisters would talk nonstop, switching from English to German if a particular German phrase fit better with the story they were telling. They would talk about family, how they spent their time, their ailments, and whose memory was not working that day. They would have supper, play cards, and have a drink. None of them were heavy drinkers, but they enjoyed, as my Mom would say, a "zip"' or, as my Dad would say, "a wee drop."

The sisters would reminisce about all the foolishness they had seen and laugh about how silly they were when the whole family, especially their husbands and brothers, were with them. They grew up listening and dancing to fiddle, accordion, mouth organ, and guitar music, and "old-time" music would play in the background as they visited. After supper, they would talk more and tease one another as they played cards and dice games until late into the evening. Then, of course, they would have what they called "a night lunch."

Mom would walk home by herself after midnight and then call Madeline to tell her she had made it to her apartment safely. They would chat for another hour after having spent the entire evening together. Mom said she would always remember to go to the bathroom prior to calling Madeline; she knew that even though they had just spent several hours together, they would talk for a long time.

This move to her apartment kept Mom connected with her sisters, and they could see each other daily if they wished. They would plan and attend outings, such as weddings, family reunions, and funerals. Reunions were their favourite. Monthly, they attended the senior night at the Park Town Hotel, where they visited with other seniors, ate lunch, had a drink, and listened to old-time music. Sometimes, they would take the bus to the casino in the afternoon or evening, where they would eat, have a drink, and play the machines. Who better to hang out with than your sisters, who had known you forever?

Mom never thought of herself as poor, but she never thought she would live in a penthouse. She had worked hard, saved her money, and sold her house. Now she could live in a beautiful apartment near her sisters. She was proud she could afford such a delightful home and have money to look after herself. Our family was happy Mom was able to live well and independently; Winnifred was Mom's money advisor and served her well.

Mom's children and grandchildren visited and would stay with Mom often. She would go on trips with family and sometimes stay with them for weeks at a time. Mom enjoyed spending time with our families and attending activities. She had been to hockey rinks, basketball courts, soccer pitches, swimming pools, dance theatres, auditoriums, and racetracks across the province and Canada. She had participated in weddings, engagements, baby showers, funerals, graduations, convocations, and many other special occasions with family. Mom was very open to trying new things and welcomed each day. Life was enjoyable.

Although Mom had lived a good, healthy life, full of love and hope, faith, and happiness, it hadn't been without hardship. Yet, somehow, her faith and prayer always saw her through the hardship, making her more resilient, stronger in faith, and ever grateful.

The year 2013 was a traumatic one for Mom. In March, her second oldest son, Wesley, only sixty-three years old, died suddenly from a heart attack while working in Prague, in the Czech Republic. He was well-recognized nationally and internationally for his contribution to continuing education and travelled all over the world with his work. When Wesley walked into a room, people took note. His presence commanded attention, and Mom was proud of him. She was thankful she could contribute to furthering his education so he could achieve his Doctor of Education, a degree which enabled him to rise further in his field. Even though he paid his mother back the tuition, he was grateful that she helped him financially at the time as the doctorate degree opened more opportunities for him to excel in the work he loved.

Mary and Wesley
2008

Wesley's death broke my heart. Only a year and a bit apart in age, we were each other's best friend growing up and were very close. He was my family partner, just as my younger sisters, WJK4 and WJK5, were family partners, and my oldest brother, WJK1, and youngest brother, WJK6, were family partners.

COURAGE AND A CASTLE

Mom was trying to come to grips with Wesley's death, but it was hard for her to comprehend, even to process some of the smaller details such as when he died. She remembered when I came to her apartment one afternoon near the end of winter and told her that Wesley had died. It was one of the most heart-wrenching things I've ever had to do. I was crying and I had to repeat several times that Wesley had died, because the news wasn't sinking in. Mom looked confused. She was unable to take in the news, no matter how I explained it. Our unconditional-love mother, who gave birth to us and nurtured us our entire lives, was unable to respond emotionally to the fact that her son had died.

For Mom, the loss did not feel real. She was in disbelief, powerless to understand the death of her son. She was numb and unable to feel any genuine emotion. She remembered that my husband and I took her to Wesley's funeral in Victoria and that she went on an airplane. She remembered seeing family at the funeral. She also recalled being upset with my husband because he got lost driving back from the viewing. Agitation was not an emotion Mom had usually displayed in the past, but it was the one she felt and showed most often now.

When we returned from my brother's celebration of life, Mom talked with her sisters and tried to explain that Wesley was gone. No matter how much she talked about it, she could not come to peace with it. She told her sisters that it was not right that a mother should bury her son, let alone a second son.

Before Wesley's passing in March 2013, our family began planning for Mom's ninetieth birthday in September of that year. One tentative plan was to take her on a trip. She had often talked about going to Hawaii, but she said she didn't want to go; Hawaii was the place she wanted to go with Dad, but he was gone, and she didn't want to go there now. We were somewhat surprised at her refusal. In retrospect, her lack of emotion, somewhat disagreeable behaviour, and agitation should have triggered that something was amiss with Mom. Still, we did not pick up on the signs.

The death of Wesley brought heartbreak and despair to our family and bewilderment to Mom. However, our family still wanted to pay tribute to Mom's ninety years of life so a party was planned at my son's house in Saskatoon. Family and friends were invited. Mom tried to be excited about her birthday party but could not. When the family talked with her about her party, a look of extreme concentration and perplexion took over her face. Once her strained facial expression set in, her body became more rigid and stiff as if she was trying to physically block out information or was afraid. She could not feel excitement these days, but she could feel fear. She had begun to have nightmares with images and voices that scared her and she didn't understand why.

Winnie Fink (sister to Mary), Mary,
Madeline Hyland (sister to Mary)
90th Birthday Garden Party
2013

Her ninetieth birthday party was a celebration of Mom and a well-lived life. A barbeque was held in the backyard of one of her grandsons on a beautiful day in early September 2013.

Three of her sisters came, as did sisters-in-law, nieces and nephews, and her children and their families. Other relatives, friends, and some of her Bessborough family came to pay tribute to Mom, whom they knew to be a kind, giving, resourceful, and loving woman from whom they drew inspiration.

Mom was anxious and felt slightly out of sorts at the party; things were somewhat off, but she could not explain what that felt like or why. Her face was tight, she clenched her jaw, and as much as she tried, she could not seem to find joy in the day. This was indeed odd for our mother.

Over the past nine months, she had become increasingly despondent, distant, and difficult to converse with. After her birthday party, she withdrew further from spending time with her sisters. Her bad dreams continued to scare her. She sometimes became disoriented; when she was doing something, she would not remember what it was. She often had to stop and think for a few minutes before her memory returned.

One of her grandsons had to reset the television remote control more often than usual as Mom could not remember which buttons to push to watch her shows. Another of her grandsons had to do extra shopping for her as she could not recall where she put her list when she got to the store. On one occasion, her grandson had shopped for her and walked into her penthouse to find her kitchen tap running and water all over the floor. He told her the sink had overflowed, and then cleaned up the water, and put away her groceries. Sometimes, she lost her balance, or her legs would not support her as she stood up or walked. I lived the closest and visited often. Although I knew about the shopping mishaps and forgetfulness from comments from my sons, I did not know about everything as she did not tell me, even though I was there frequently trying to organize additional home support for her.

One afternoon, I asked Mom to explain to me how she knew what pills to take and when to take them. She only had four medications and two vitamins. She brought her seven-day pill box and set it on the kitchen table. I opened it to see no particular order for the different coloured pills in the little compartments. She explained at length how her system worked. I could not understand it, and by the time she finished, neither could she.

"Well then, Mom, I said, "how about we go to the pharmacy now and have your medications organized into individual bubble packs and I teach you how to use them? Then, you don't have to sort your pills out from the bottles into the little compartments."

"Alright then, we can go, but before my show, and I have to get a newspaper on the way back," Mom said, caving begrudgingly, knowing from the look on my face I was not letting this issue go.

The newspaper was significant to Mom as she liked to read it from front to back, cutting out any articles that caught her eye. At one time, she used to do the Find-a-Word puzzles in the newspaper; however, when she moved to her penthouse, one of the grandchildren gave her a computer and monitor. It was downloaded with card games; Mom learned how to play card games on the computer at seventy-eight.

Then, in her mid-eighties, her computer was replaced by a tablet with both card games and word search puzzles. She learned how to use the tablet, but still liked to cut out and attempt to complete the Find-a-Word puzzles from the newspaper. I admired how open to learning and change she was throughout her life. (The way she did her Find-a-Word puzzles always amazed me. I am unsure how she knew she was done, as she circled single letters rather than complete words. But it worked for her and kept her mind active.)

In any case, we did buy a newspaper on the way home from the pharmacy, and Mom did learn how to use the bubble-packed medication with the pharmacist's and family members' assistance.

One afternoon in early December 2013, I received a call from my oldest son, who had been checking in on Little Gram while I was in Edmonton for a special work event. When my son arrived home from work, he had a message from his grandmother telling him to call her. When he called her back, she told him she could not turn her TV on and asked him to come and fix it. He said that when he arrived, she was behaving oddly.

She was bewildered and unstable on her feet. She knew who she was, where she was, and who he was, but was disoriented. He was concerned and offered to stay with her until I could get there to check her out. As he could not stay overnight, he arranged for his daughter to come and sit with her great-grandmother until I could get there. He didn't think she should be left on her own. After this discussion with my son, my husband and I decided that we would cut our trip short so I could check on my mother sooner.

When my husband and I arrived home from Edmonton, I left him at our acreage near Shellbrook and headed immediately to Saskatoon. It was minus 30 and the time was close to 2 a.m. when I finally arrived at Mom's home.

As I drove, I feared what was happening to my

mother. She had been experiencing a bit of instability when walking on uneven surfaces, and after a visit to the doctor, I got her a walker. The first one I bought had wheels and a seat to rest on, like her sister's, the Queen. Later, Mom reported to my sister, Winnifred, that she had used her new walker to go to the grocery store across the street. It was a big event for Mom, the first trip with her new walker, a walker just like the Queen's. But suddenly, all hell broke loose. In the mall parking lot, Mom lost control of the walker. It twirled her around in circles until she was dizzy. She let go of the handles and fell to the ground. Although she had some scrapes from her fall, she wasn't seriously hurt. Somehow, she pushed the walker home and called my sister, who told her not to use it anymore.

Of course, my sister then called me. Mom had great relationships with her children, and each connection was different. Mom would tell one of my sisters something that she would never tell me, knowing that her daughters would share the information with her other children.

When I learned about Mom's perilous journey with the new Queen-like walker, I promptly returned it, despite Mom's pleas that she would learn to use it. I traded the fancy walker for one with tiny wheels you lift and push. Much safer for Mom. She was upset with me for a long time that she could not have a Queen's walker. She generally just pushed her push-and-lift walker, which might have been her way of retaliating for not having the one she wanted.

Mom did not give up on her goal to own a walker like the Queen. She still admired the Queen's walker and, over the next few years, on three different occasions, was shrewd enough to convince Home Care staff that she could use one. Then I intervened, and the Queen's walker was once more replaced with the push-and-lift type, which Mom just pushed. Sometimes, I was the bad guy.

When I arrived, I pushed the walker issue out of mind, focusing on my mother's condition. As I entered, I found my granddaughter and Mother sitting in the living room having tea. Both looked like they needed sleep. My granddaughter said, "Little Gram has been in and out of bed, saying she doesn't want to sleep because of her bad dreams. She talked a lot, but I couldn't understand everything she was saying." Seeing her great-grandmother so confused and unsteady on her feet saddened my granddaughter. I thanked her for staying and she left. Mom finished her tea and I told her it was bedtime.

As I tucked Mom into bed, I wondered what was happening to my dear mother. She looked at me as if I had just appeared this minute. "What are you doing here in the middle of the night?" she asked.

I replied, "Tucking you into bed. You must rest now, and we will talk in the morning."

I left her room, and when I returned to check on her a few minutes later, I saw that she was not in bed. I found her in the spare room, face down, stretched out on the floor and unable to get up. She struggled to push herself into a sitting position, but her legs would not cooperate. She was scared; her eyes were deep and dark with fear and confusion. Mom did not know how she got to the spare room, how she came to be on the floor, or why she could not get up off the floor. I tried to speak to her in a soothing voice, though I was horrified that she had fallen and could not get up. After some reassurance that her legs might work now, Mom tried to stand. Her legs worked and I supported her as she slowly and carefully took baby steps to her bed.

Now, we were both confused about what was happening with her. I sat at her bedside, talking with her as I covered her up, instructing her to call out to me if she needed to get out of bed, and I would come. Mom was exhausted. She said her prayers and drifted off to sleep.

In the morning, Mom was clear-minded. She could talk, walk, and move about without difficulty or pain. Luckily, she had no bruises from the fall. We discussed how she was feeling and what was happening to her. She agreed that she should see a doctor. I made an appointment.

In the early afternoon, Mom wanted to get money. She always liked having cash in her wallet and said she had none. Though the bank in the mall was only across the street, it was minus 30 so I drove. We were walking in the mall when Mom suddenly could no longer walk. Her legs would not work; no matter how hard she tried, she could not move them. We were near a bench, so I half dragged her to it. Mom was frightened and distressed that her legs were not working. I was frightened and distressed too.

I instructed her to stay sitting on the bench and wait for me. I went and bought a wheelchair from a shop at the other end of the mall. I considered the difficulty in transferring Mom back and forth from the wheelchair to the car twice. So, even though it was still minus 30, I bundled her up and quickly wheeled her home across the street. We were not home long when Mom found she could stand and walk again. What the hell!

The Christmas Miracle

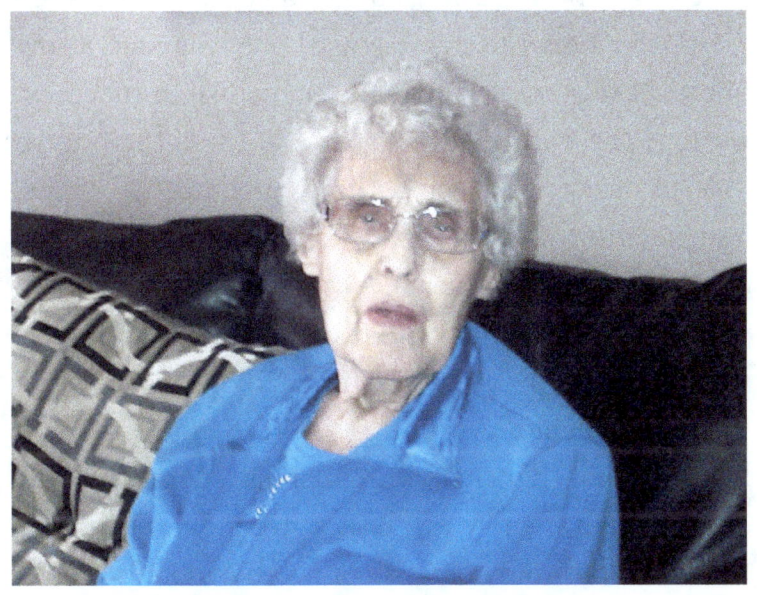

Mary
October 2013

COURAGE AND A CASTLE

When you believe in God and have faith, miracles can happen.

I took Mom to see her doctor the next day. The initial examination found nothing out of the ordinary, but the doctor ordered diagnostic tests to be completed in the following days.

I was concerned for Mom's safety and health, so I took her home to my acreage. She was safe at my house. It was comfortable and home-like in the forest setting. She had her own room and I was there to be able to assist with her bathing, prepare her meals, and generally pamper her.

Mom was never a sit-in-your-chair-with-your-feet-up lady of leisure and filled all her waking hours with productive activity even if she wasn't at home. As she aged, the intensity and frequency of her help diminished. More recently, she would help with less strenuous activities like dusting, sweeping floors, and doing dishes — and, of course, making homemade soup for my husband. As time went on, at her own home, she became a bit more comfortable with having some household tasks completed for her, but she continued to live independently.

The onset of her new condition, where she had no interest in communicating and was uncertain if she could walk from one minute to the next, was perplexing for her family. However, Mom didn't know she was so unwell nor did she recall that she had always been an active person — therefore, she was fine with just sitting, resting, and being looked after.

Mom still enjoyed playing cards with my family and listening to her old-time music. At mealtimes, the dog would sit beside the table under Mom's walker and Mom would put her hand on the walker and drop anything she did not want to eat. The dog would happily consume whatever Mom offered. I would say, "Ma, don't give the dog all your food."

She would look me in the eye and say, "I am not feeding the dog my supper," while her outstretched hand continued to drop food for the dog.

I can't explain why we had the same conversation daily, as she was fully aware she was feeding the dog and was fine telling me she wasn't. Clearly the dog was the winner.

Christmas was drawing near, the holiday Mom loved most. The family would gather at the acreage with gifts, food, drinks, cards, and music. Mom tried to be excited about Christmas, but it was hard for her to connect emotionally or understand what was happening around her. Sometimes, her conversation was clear and on topic. Other times, she spoke only a few words, leaving the other person to guess the message. Sometimes she was able to move about with her walker quite easily, and other days, I would have to push her in her wheelchair. What her mobility depended on at any given moment, I could not tell.

The tests the doctor ordered a few weeks earlier showed nothing that could provide a diagnosis, and Mom was referred to a specialist. Unfortunately, due to the holiday season, it would be the new year before Mom would have that next appointment.

Sometimes, Mom found it hard to sleep at night. She was afraid she would have bad dreams. I would tuck her into bed and leave the music on for her to fall asleep. It seemed to calm her. However, after sleeping briefly, Mom would awaken and sneak out of bed to get something. She was never sure what she intended to get, only that she had to get out of bed. I would often come to check on her, and to my distress, find her lying on the floor beside her bed. I would scold her for getting out of bed without assistance, but my efforts were futile. Mom did not understand why I was scolding her. She did not understand why her legs were not always functioning, or why she had such terrible dreams. She did not know why she could not remember many things or feel emotions. None of the doctors we had seen so far could explain what was happening.

One evening, I gave Mom a bell to ring and a whistle to blow, two ways to call me if she needed something. I also instructed her not to get out of bed by herself. That strategy did not work as Mom could not remember she was not to get out of bed by herself and ignored the bell and whistle. So, I began to do frequent night checks and often found her with one leg out of the bed, ready to step to the floor.

In desperation, one night, I tied Christmas bells onto the blankets by Mom's feet to alert me if she was attempting to get out of bed. The subsequent bed check resulted in my finding Mom sitting up, quietly and carefully, trying to untie the bells so she could get out of bed without my knowing. I was amazed and amused. I scolded Mom for undoing the bells and trying to get out of bed, and then could not help but laugh at the situation's absurdity. We both laughed.

After our laughter, I said, "Move over, Ma."

"Why?" she asked.

I said, "I don't know what else to do, so I am sleeping with you so you can't get out of bed and hurt yourself."

Mom moved over and gave a half smile, not knowing if this was good or bad. And that became the routine: Mom and I were sleeping together, her sleeping on the side of the bed against the wall and me on the outside.

Mom was no longer her usual Christmas-loving self. The house was decorated for Christmas without her involvement. She was content to rest in her room while listening to her music, to sit at the kitchen table and do her puzzles, or to recline in a chair in the living room and look at the Christmas tree or watch the forest surrounding the house. I did very little Christmas baking; a task that in the past, Mom loved to help with. But this year, she had no energy, and had no interest in Christmas. Her confusion came and went, as did her ability to walk. Although she would respond if you talked to her, she was withdrawn and communicating less. I was distressed at the condition of her health and my inability to be able to change it.

On Christmas Eve, the family arrived, lunch was served, and gifts were opened. Mom did not smile as she was helped to open her gifts. She wanted to go to her room, rest in bed, and listen to her music. Normally, a few of us would take Mom to midnight mass, but there was no midnight mass that year as Little Gram was not up to travelling even a short distance.

On Christmas Day, more relatives arrived, and Mom became more withdrawn; the overwhelm of sounds and activity was making her anxious.

Mom had her usual place for Christmas dinner at the table to my left. As we ate, she slumped over to the left. The family noted that something was off with Little Gram and tried to keep her included in the conversations as usual. However, she spoke only a few words and made hand gestures, pointing at items she wanted like salt or water.

The typical Christmas meal of turkey, potatoes, gravy, ham, and cabbage rolls was served. Mom loved mashed potatoes and gravy, but she had been eating very little these past days, with much of her food going to the smiling dog who sat under her walker. I dished up a plate for her with a bit of everything she liked. Mom started to eat with her knife. I took away the knife and gave her a fork. Mom put the fork down and picked up a spoon. After a few mouthfuls using the spoon, Mom put the spoon down and began to scoop up her mashed potatoes and gravy with her fingers, and put them in her mouth. My grandchildren later said they were amazed that Little Gram didn't get a slap from me for eating with her fingers. Instead, I fed her the rest of her supper. What she did not want to swallow, she spat out. After supper, while sitting at the table, Mom began to slouch. She could hardly sit up, so she was put to bed for a rest.

Once most of the family left, my husband, my adult daughter and I discussed whether or not Little Gram should be taken to emergency at the hospital in Prince Albert. The final straw in making that determination was when my daughter checked on Mom, who was resting in my bed. Little Gram had her legs pulled tightly into her chest and was rocking in a fetal position. She was speaking words that were not recognizable and seemed to be in another language. I knew then that we could not wait another minute to get her to the hospital.

I was apprehensive and fearful; I had no idea what was happening to Mom and was sure that whatever it was, it would be fatal. I wanted to keep my mother as long as I could. I was afraid that the Christmas we just celebrated would be the last one I would ever have with her. It was minus 35 and I bundled Mom up in a winter coat, boots, mittens and scarf and wrapped a blanket around her. My husband carried her frail body to the car. I sat in the back seat with her.

Mom was talking to me, but it was as if she was speaking in tongues. Finally, I said, "Ma, I am listening really hard to understand, but I can't comprehend what you are saying."

Mom's reply was clear, "I can't understand what I am saying either."

We both laughed, but we were both frightened by this new symptom.

Mom went back to speaking in tongues.

At the hospital in Prince Albert, tests, including a scan, were done. Mom had a brain bleed. The good news was that they could fix it! The doctor said all they had to do was *drill a hole* in her skull and drain off the blood! This was shocking news on two levels. First, the doctor needed to drill a hole in my mother's head; second, her condition *could* be rectified. You cannot imagine the shock and joy my husband and I experienced when we heard the doctor say Mom could be fixed! This would certainly be a miracle if Little Gram could be made well again.

The doctor said that as Mom was only ninety and in good health, she should be able to survive the surgery and carry on for a few more years of healthy living. He explained that all her recent symptoms were a result of the pooled blood putting pressure on various parts of the brain. This explained her confusion, the sudden inability to walk, her speaking in gibberish, her inability to understand or feel emotions, and the onset of her nightmares. The doctor said that Mom would not be as good as new, but she would return to where she was before the brain bleed began. When we asked what would have been the cause for the brain bleed, he said that it was likely a result of a fall where she probably hit her head.

The doctor arranged for Mom to spend the night in the Prince Albert hospital and to be transported by ambulance to the Royal University Hospital in Saskatoon the following morning. My husband and I went home where I had a few hours of sleep before I went back to the hospital to follow Mom's ambulance to Saskatoon.

I reported Mom's condition and the doctor's diagnosis and prognosis to my siblings. They were as shocked as I that Mom could be fixed. Just cut a hole in her head!

But like me, they were worried. They didn't want to lose their precious Mom. *Is Mom going to make it?* they all asked. I *don't know,* was my answer.

None of my siblings could join me at the hospital as one was out of Canada, and the other two lived on opposite sides of the country. So, we agreed no one would make arrangements to come until we knew the results of the surgery. Everyone would pray for Mom and I would let them know how it went.

On Boxing Day, another minus 35 morning, Mom was taken from the Prince Albert Hospital to Royal University Hospital in Saskatoon by ambulance. I followed the ambulance in my own vehicle. At the hospital in Saskatoon, I saw Mom briefly before she was taken for surgery. She was unresponsive, but was no longer curled into a fetal position as she had been when I left the hospital a handful of hours before. Thanks to medication, her body was relaxed; she was laying on her back with a blanket covering her to her chest, her uncovered arms and hands by her sides. She made no movement, but I could see her chest slowly rise and fall as she breathed. Her eyes stared off into the distance, blinking infrequently, expressionless and empty, blank like her face, void of all knowing and feeling.

I stroked her face and told her I was there, and we were all praying for her. I showed her one of her favorite rosaries that I brought with me. I told her the doctors said that they were hopeful that they could help her. I kissed her on the cheek. "I love you, Mom. I will be right here when you get out of surgery."

I waited anxiously at the hospital. I talked to my family. My siblings were waiting and praying for a positive outcome. I paced, I sat, I thought. I held Mom's rosary in my hand from time to time and then placed it back in my pocket.

Prayer using the rosary often brought Mom what she needed. Although I am not a religious person, I am a spiritual one. I felt the presence of both of my deceased brothers while I waited. I believed they were signaling that Mom would be okay. I did not feel my dad's presence; he would be with Mom.

It felt like an eternity. Finally, the doctor appeared and reported that the surgery had been successfully performed without complications. What a blessing and relief for our family that Mom had come through the surgery! I called my husband and my children and one sister who contacted the rest of the family. Little Gram, Mom, would be okay. Mom must have talked directly to the Lord, and he let her stay with us! We were all elated.

Mom was taken to a recovery area. After a while, she was moved to another location where I could sit with her. I felt a mixture of anxiety and happiness as I entered the hospital room. I had no idea what to expect. Mom was still, covered with a flannel sheet to her shoulders. I could see the sheet slowly moving up and down to the rhythm of her breathing. *Excellent*, I thought. Her eyes were closed. A thick, white, blood-stained bandage was wrapped around her tiny head. A tube draining blood from her head poked out from under the bandage. There were tubes in her arms hooked up to a machine.

I sighed with relief. Mom was alive! I gently kissed her on the cheek, touched her hands — which were cold as usual — and sat in a chair by her bed. I was exhausted and relieved. I wept.

After some time, Mom awoke and began speaking in short but rational sentences — in English! I was over the moon! She said she was not in any pain but was very sleepy. I placed her rosary in her hand. She said someone must have been saying Hail Marys, and we both smiled. She closed her eyes and slept.

Doctor's orders were that she remain on bed rest

that day. I stayed with her as she slept the rest of the afternoon and evening. When I was confident enough that Mom would be all right, I left to spend the night at her apartment, where I had my first restful sleep in many nights.

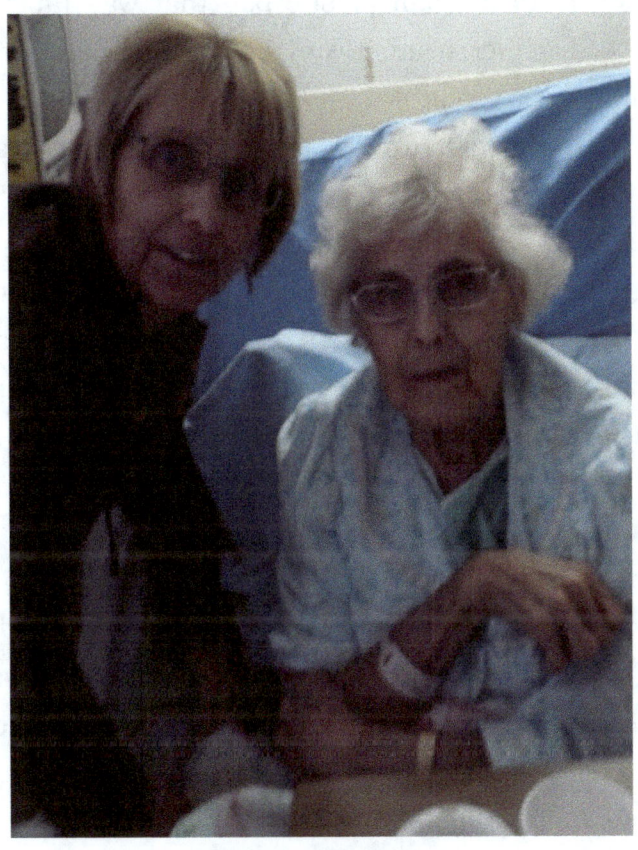

Mary and Wanita
at the University Hospital after Mary's brain surgery
Saskatoon – December 2013

The next morning, my husband came to my mom's apartment, and we went to the hospital together. When we arrived at the hospital, Mom was awake and lying quietly in bed. The large white bandage had been replaced with a smaller one. It covered the shaved part of her head. Only the tube draining blood from her head remained. It was connected to a small plastic bag that was taped to the back of her head. Even the IV tubes and other monitors were gone.

When I spoke to her, she sat up in bed and responded like her usual ninety-year-old self. We were carrying on a logical conversation. Wow! I hadn't had a real conversation with Mom for months. Now she was back, present in body and mind and talking with me as she did before she got sick. My heart was happy.

I asked her how she felt, and she said, "I feel good. Look." She stepped out of bed and marched smartly around the room while swinging her arms back and forth at her sides. When she returned to her bed, she spun around, threw her arms toward the sky as if saying "Ta Da!" Then she said, "There, I can do that." My husband and I stood motionless, stunned. Tears streamed down our faces. We were in awe as we watched Mom's miraculous demonstration. Mom was back! What a fantastic "Christmas Miracle."

Mom never did fully recall the events before Christmas that led to her having brain surgery. However, she did remember speaking in tongues, which always brought a smile to her face. She understood German and knew some Hungarian but was fully aware that the language she spoke the evening we went to the hospital was neither German nor any other language she knew.

Mary
weekend at the acreage
May 2014

Mom was a woman of faith and believed in God. She was a woman who loved to pray, especially the rosary. She lived a life of faith, love, and servitude. Her siblings and children lovingly refer to her as "Holy Mary" and believed she had a special connection to the saints and the Lord. This unique connection to the Lord proved authentic, as evidenced by what the family calls the "Christmas Miracle."

Our family was overjoyed to have our mother, the family matriarch, fondly known as "Holy Mary," "Little Gram," or "Grandma Mary," share seven more Christmases. We are still grateful for Mary's Christmas Miracle.

When you believe in God and have faith, miracles can happen.

You Are My Sunshine

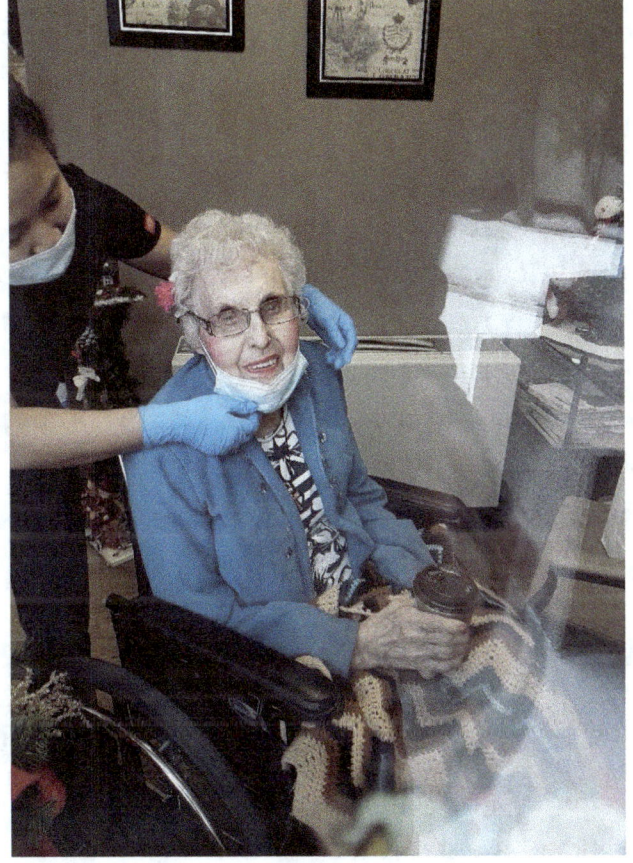

Mary
with one of her care home staff
2020

During her recovery, it became clear that Mom could no longer live alone. Though she had times when her physical and mental capacity were similar to before her surgery, her short-term memory had not returned as much as anticipated, nor had her mobility. She could not live without some assistance; not only did she walk with a walker, she also needed help with daily tasks. The family agreed that Mom needed more care, and a personal care home was the best option.

From a distance, my sister assisted with identifying care homes in Saskatoon to investigate, but once we realized it would be easier for me to engage in meaningful daily contact with Mom if she lived closer to me, the hunt for an appropriate personal care home shifted from Saskatoon to Prince Albert.

I had always told my sisters that Mom would live with me when she could no longer live alone; I did not want her in a care home. Mom had her own view and often teased our family, "I don't have to worry when I am old; Wanita will look after me at Pine Grove." Pine Grove is the Provincial Women's Correctional Centre where I worked at that time. Mom said, "The ladies are well looked after there, and I can have my own room." This brought howls of laughter from my sisters.

However, as much as I once thought it would be

best for Mom to live with me, I could not make that happen without quitting work. Therefore, Mom had to go into a care home.

The minus 30 temperatures had made touring care homes brutal. Wanda and I had daily discussions about which personal care homes we were comfortable with Mom living in. I would then make appointments to go and talk to the care home owner and tour the facility. I visited several homes in Saskatoon, but once we decided it was better to move Mom to Prince Albert, I started all over — touring potential personal care homes once Wanda had identified them as possibilities.

The facility we preferred had a wait list so we found a suitable interim home while we waited for Mom to be accepted at our preferred location. Once we had a date in mid-January for Mom to move to the care home, my sisters made plans to come to Saskatoon and finish sorting out Mom's belongings and pack up her apartment. They would then bring her from the hospital in Saskatoon directly to the care home in Prince Albert.

We discussed bringing Mom to my house for tea or supper before we took her to the care home. Although all of us thought it was a great idea and Mom would love it as she loved being at the acreage, we thought Mom might refuse to leave once she was at my house. So, we decided to take her directly to the care home.

While Mom was ill, most of December and January, the temperature was a frigid minus 35; looking at potential places for Mom to live, visiting her at the hospital, keeping watch on her apartment, and preparing for moving in such cold weather was hard on my body and mind. In mid-January 2014, my two sisters came to visit Mom, who was still hospitalized, and then began the job of cleaning Mom's apartment and sorting her life's treasures. When the day came to transfer Mom from the hospital to her new home, they agreed that they would physically take Mom to the care home. I was so grateful; I could not bear to take her there myself. I agreed to come later in the day once Mom was settled.

The transition was difficult for Mom as she wanted to continue living independently. However, as time passed, she began to recognize her limitations and embraced this new life chapter.

Her initial placement was in an older care home in a residential neighbourhood near where I used to live before we moved out to the country. Although it was older, it was clean. Few residents had their own bathroom; Mom had to share a bathroom with three others. Her room was tiny, but she said it felt like her bedroom when she lived on Avenue T North in Saskatoon, which she found comforting.

Eighteen months later, when I told Mom that she would be moving to a new care home, the one we preferred, she said she would not. She had come to know the staff and residents and liked it where she was.

I took her to tour the new care home. Each spacious bedroom had its own bathroom; the new care home was clean and inviting with a large open area for dining and activities. It also had a beautiful yard for sitting in the sun. Despite the fact that she would have loved this home when she first moved to Prince Albert, Mom was not impressed. Eventually, she humoured me and agreed to the move. As time passed, she came to like the staff and residents, even more than her old place.

Unfortunately, two years after she moved in, the owner of the care home sold the facility Mom was living in, necessitating a move to a new facility. We thought the transition would go well as the same owner and staff would manage the care home Mom was transitioning to. However, despite the new location being a brand-new facility, Mom was not at all excited and said that moving was a silly idea.

The owner had sold the building to a Catholic

Order as a residence for a group of nuns. Mom was annoyed that she would have to move out so the nuns could move in. "Why do the nuns have to move into my care home?" she demanded to know. "They should get a different place!"

This was the reaction from my Catholic mother. It was out of character; certainly in the past, she would not have been one to complain, so vocally and vehemently, and especially not about Catholic nuns! She moved, but not without a grumbling protest.

After some time in the newly built care home, Mom accepted it as home. She would often tell people that she was well cared for. The new care home was big and clean, with large dining rooms and living rooms on each of the four floors and a huge gathering place on the lower level facing the river. Special events for the residents were held there, such as the Mother's Day Tea and the Christmas party, with families invited to attend. But Mom often told me that she still wished she could have stayed in the place the nuns bought. Those damn nuns! But, as was characteristic of Mom, she eventually adjusted to the change and still enjoyed each new day.

At her care home, she came to be known by staff as their "Social Butterfly." Our family found this interesting. Mom had little time for socializing and friends while she worked full-time at the

Bessborough Hotel and raised six children — she was always family-focused, and free-from-work time was spent with family and extended family.

Once she retired, she had time to volunteer at St. Mary's Church and joined the Catholic Women's League. Mom enjoyed baking desserts for church functions and helping serve lunches and fall suppers. Attending Sunday Mass and all the special masses was a priority for her. Christmas and Easter masses were her favourites. Mom listened to the *Saturday Night Dance Party*, an old-time music program on the radio, and spent time with her sisters, her Bessborough friends, and our families. She was a vibrant and busy woman, but her family would never have called her a "social butterfly."

Now, at the care home in Prince Albert, Mom could not spend her days with her sisters, family or church — the cornerstones of her life in Saskatoon. So she adapted, taking her circumstances as another of her life's opportunities.

At the care home, Mom participated in all the daily activities. Staff would remind her of what was on the schedule and she would happily join in the events such as Bingo, exercise, crafts, and daily tea in the morning and afternoon.

As agreeable as she was with many of the staff's instructions, she was so not agreeable with twice-a-week baths and would give in to the second weekly bath only after the staff reminded her that "The Boss" insisted she have two baths weekly. She would ask them, "Who is the Boss over me?"

Mary
93rd Birthday
2016

They would reply, "It is your daughter, Wanita." She would agree that her daughter was "The Boss" but remarked further that she did not know how I got to be "The Boss" over her and her baths.

She enjoyed socializing with the residents outside of the planned activities as well. Playing cards with the other ladies in the dining room was the highlight of her day.

Mom looked forward to Mass when the priest came and the weekly meeting of the residents' Rosary prayer group. Mom especially enjoyed the music and singers who came to entertain at the care home. She still liked listening to her old-time music. The care home was now her home.

Mom was still included in family events and liked to go to the lake and out to our acreage near Prince Albert. (Our acreage was near Holbein, about 15 minutes from Shellbrook and 25 minutes from Prince Albert.) Her youngest daughters, Winnifred and Wanda, who lived in other provinces, came to visit several times a year. Sometimes, they would stay with her at the care home in a special room for the family. Other times, they would bring Mom to our acreage and spend time with her there. Wayne, also living out of province, spent a week with her at the acreage after her ninety-third birthday.

Despite Alzheimer's, Mom was pleasant and maintained her keen sense of humor. She was a respectful, kind, humble woman with a positive outlook. Each day was welcomed with genuine gratitude and anticipation of promising daily activities. The staff would assist her with any tasks she needed help with to ready herself for the day. Her daughters bought her many outfits and clothes, so she had a large wardrobe to choose from. The staff helped Mom to select a fresh outfit for the day and helped her dress. On days when the hairdresser did not style her hair, the staff would do it for her. They put rouge on her cheeks and red lipstick on her lips. Lipstick and rouge were refreshed for her before each meal. Mom never had time to get her nails done while working and rarely wore nail polish, but now every Friday at her care home, while she enjoyed a glass of wine, her nails were trimmed and polished her favourite bright red.

However, Mom was growing more vocal about her likes and dislikes. Her lifetime preferences seemed to change; for example, she now said she never drank coffee, and she would not take it if you offered her a cup. However, in reality, Mom had drunk coffee all her life and preferred it to tea. But now she only drank tea. Her memory of her likes and dislikes and what she used to do was becoming blurred. Her ability to understand and process information was diminishing. Mom would often ask, "What do I do now?" More and more frequently, her memory failed her.

Fortunately, her love of music and prayer remained constant, and she listened to her music of polkas and waltzes and prayed daily by herself and with her son via telephone. She had worn out two Bibles through her years of prayer with Wayne. When it was time for a third one, I printed out the prayers in large print in the order that they read them together, then inserted them into plastic sheets in a binder. It was straightforward for Mom to follow, to just flip the pages and pray with Wayne. Her prayer time with her son and the Rosary were dear to her.

The care home staff were genuinely fond of Mom and took excellent care of her. She was not high maintenance despite needing assistance with many daily tasks. She appreciated the staff's help and companionship and expressed her gratitude to them often.

While they were helping her with her daily tasks, they would talk with her. Mom liked that. They would talk about her life and her family. They put on her old-time music, and she would tap her toes as she sang along with such performers as Don Messer and Frankie Yankovic. She liked to dance. It was not unusual for her to keep the beat to her music as she walked along with her walker. It made the staff smile to see Mom enjoying herself and her music. When they entered her room, whether it was for cleaning or personal care, staff members would listen to the lyrics and sing along with Mom.

Mary and Wayne
Wanita's acreage
2017

In the past, Mom only sang in earshot of close family as she didn't think she had a good singing voice. She would sing to us children at bedtime. One of my fondest memories is of Mom singing

You Are My Sunshine to me when I was little. She occasionally called me "Sunshine," even once I was an adult. After some years, I realized Mom sang the same song to all her children and called all of us "Sunshine." We took it as a beautiful term of endearment.

With memory loss, Mom no longer remembered that she didn't think she had a good singing voice and frequently sang with staff, other residents, or even just to herself.

At the care home, she called the staff members "Sunshine" as they were like family to her. It was common to find Mom sitting on the bed chatting with the staff, a flower from the weekly bouquet Wanda sent her tucked in her freshly combed hair.

The care aide would ask, "Mary, what is your favorite song?"

She would reply, "You Are My Sunshine."

The care aide would say, "Sing it with me," and they would burst into the song together. Mom always enjoyed the care staff singing along with her. She would sing, smile, and sway side to side as they sang.

Once, I went to visit Mom and found no one in her room, but I did hear voices coming from the bathroom. The care staff member was helping Mom use the washroom and they were chatting. Suddenly, I heard a thunderous version of "You Are My

Sunshine" sung by the two of them, coming through the bathroom door. They finished the song, stopped for a brief chit-chat, and started the song over again as if practicing for a duet. What a beautiful time they were having.

I treasure that moment, hearing Mom sing one of her favourite songs and the staff person singing happily along, enjoying their time together. I felt comfort and joy, knowing that Mom was well cared for and genuinely loved by those who looked after her. Mom gave and received much "Sunshine" while she was alive — and the "sun" still "shines" for all those who knew and loved her.

Shades of Mary

Mary, aka "Mafia Mama"
September 2019

COURAGE AND A CASTLE

Mom and I were off to her denturist — for the second time in two weeks. The week before, we had left the care home with good intentions, but had inadvertently left her walker behind, requiring a second visit in as many weeks. This time, we had the walker and I would be able to transfer her from her wheelchair to the dental chair successfully.

We made our usual stop to pick up tea for me and caffé mocha for Mom. No Timbits this morning before the appointment as she would not be able to clean her mouth before seeing the denturist. I ran in and picked up our order, leaving the booklet, *Our Daily Bread*, for Mom to read. In the past, she would complete Find-a-Word puzzles when we travelled, but now she struggled to complete the puzzles in book form, even though she had adapted to doing the puzzles on her tablet. We didn't bring her tablet on today's adventure, so she read her prayer booklet while alone in the car. (I had learned to put her purse out of her sight and reach when I left her alone in the car. Otherwise, she would take out her wallet and count her money — an action that could attract attention; I had previously caught ne'er-do-wells standing at her car window, trying to convince her to open the window or the door.)

Soon, we started our journey, listening to Calvin Vollrath's version of *Maple Sugar*, a song which got

Mom's toes tapping. She hummed and sang along, occasionally stopping to ask or tell me something. She was excited about our trip.

"Did you remember to bring my walker?" she asked.

I smiled and said, "Yes, I remembered this time."

We both laughed because, generally, she was the one with memory problems.

I parked underground at the Midtown Plaza. Mom was helpful in moving into her wheelchair. She tucked her purse tightly under her left arm as she always did.

I pushed the wheelchair, the straps of my purse and a personal care bag for Mom over my shoulder.

The building and the denturist's office were wheelchair accessible, so we could easily move about. At the counter, I asked the denturist's receptionist, "Can I leave Mom here while I go to the car and get her walker so she can transfer into the dental chair?"

"Of course, I will keep an eye on Miss Mary," she replied.

"Thank you," I replied and told Mom, "Mom, I will be right back. Don't go away."

She gave me a puzzled smile and said, "Where would I go?"

Miss Mary, I thought, as I walked back to the car. I wondered whether the receptionist called all her elderly patients in that manner or whether Mom's surname — Koczka — was just too much of a mouthful.

I was only back a minute when the receptionist called, "Miss Mary, come with me, please."

I pushed Mom's wheelchair into the dental examination area and then fetched her walker. When I returned, I found the denturist asking Mom about how her mouth felt, how her teeth fit, and her ability to chew certain foods, and Mom provided relevant responses. After making some notes, the denturist smiled and turned to Mom, "Okay, let's move you into the dental chair. Then you can give me your teeth, and I will check them and your mouth. I see you have your walker so we can transfer you today."

Mom smiled and offered, "My daughter forgot the walker last week, and we had to come back again today."

"I remember. Sometimes good help is hard to find," she teased.

"Yes, good daughters are hard to find sometimes as well," Mom quipped back with a smile. Mom was pleased that she remembered how to tease.

We moved Mom from her wheelchair to the dental chair without incident. Once Mom was comfortable, the assistant selected a pair of brown glasses with enormous frames, removed Miss

Mary's glasses and gently placed the oversized dark sunglasses on her face to protect her eyes during the examination. Mom was a bit confused as she could not see well without her glasses, and these sunglasses were so dark they further impaired her vision. Once the examination was complete, the denturist left the room to make adjustments on the dentures, leaving Mom in the chair, dark glasses still in place.

I looked out the window and said, "Ma, when you get your glasses back on, I will take you to the window, and you can see the Bessborough Hotel where you used to work." She did not respond, so I turned toward her, and what I saw made me laugh out loud.

My mother was half-asleep, stretched out on the reclined dentist's chair in her dark brown outfit with pearl-like sequins decorating the neckline, her light brown jacket opened to the sides, and the enormous brown sunglasses covering her eyes. Her mouth was closed tightly.

My first thought was that she looked like a wealthy Mafia lady. With her glittery shirt and dark sunglasses, she could be Tony Soprano's mother. Her relaxed yet authoritative demeanour was such that the gangsters would be compelled to atone if she commanded them. I certainly would not want to mess with her. The scenario amused me, so I photographed my Mafia mother. When I laughed, she stirred. She looked at me questioningly and I said, "Ma, the way you were laying in the chair with the dark glasses and all, you look like a tough Mafia lady to me."

She just smiled.

The denturist reappeared. Miss Mary's dentures were returned and now fit nicely. The enormous dark glasses that turned my gentle and kind mother into the Mafia lady were removed and replaced with her glasses. My mother, was back.

I helped her to the window with her walker to view the stately Bessborough Hotel. Seeing the impressive hotel brought bits of lost memories, and she smiled and began, "I used to work there, at that beautiful castle?" First, asking, then recalling, "Yes. I worked there many years."

"Almost thirty, "I said.

"Thirty is a long time. How long have I been retired?" she asked.

"Almost thirty years as well," I responded.

"I guess I worked a long time so I could retire a long time."

"I guess you did. You worked hard, and now you can relax."

"I liked working at The Bessborough; it is a beautiful hotel. I always loved it."

"Me too, Ma. How about I leave you by the front desk, take the walker back to the car, come back for you, and then we can go shopping and have lunch."

"That's fine," she agreed, then asked, "Can I have *Wong Tong* soup?"

"For sure you can," I said.

It was close to lunchtime when we finished the appointment. We planned to have lunch at the new food court in the mall. I knew they served Wonton soup. We were having a great day so far.

Along the way, we stopped at one of Mom's favourite ladies' wear stores to see if there were any outfits she might like. I maneuvered her wheelchair around the store, and she pointed out pants and tops that she liked. The clerk asked if Mom wanted to try them on. Mom told her, "My daughter will try them on for me. We are similar in size."

So, Mom sat in her wheelchair as I went in and out of the dressing room trying on outfits. She liked how the pants looked and fitted me, so those went in the "Yes" pile. After seeing the tops on me, she decided none of them were to her liking. The helpful clerk was amused at our shopping method. I paid for Mom's pants, and she said, "I have money. I can pay." And continued, "Okay, if you pay, you can just take money from me; you know how to do that."

"Yes, Mom," I said.

"You are not going to take my money, are you? I don't think you ever do," she added.

"Mom, you have looked after me my whole life. Now it's my turn to look after you when I can."

"You always say that." She sighed contently and we moved through the hallway to the food court.

Mom reminded me that she was hungry, specifically for Wonton soup — or Wong Tong soup, as she called it. She enjoyed Wonton soup, and as they never served at her care home, we often ordered it when were out together.

The bowl of tasty broth with wonton noodles was huge and Mom couldn't eat it all. So, the remaining soup was taken with us for her to eat back at her care home. Her offer to pay for lunch was politely declined.

On the way out of town, we went through the drive-through. Tea for me and caffé mocha and Timbits for Mom. Her familiar music, humming and singing, filled the car as we started our journey home. But soon, Miss Mary's head nodded forward as sleep overtook her. Her caffé mocha and Timbits remained untouched. The drive home was pleasant and comforting, with the old-time music playing and the occasional soft snoring from Mom.

While I drove, I thought, *What a Mother I have. Life is always an adventure with her.* I was still captivated by the sight of Mom wearing the large, dark glasses, being transformed into a woman who resembled a wealthy, Mafia lady. How I love my mother and Miss Mary, I mused. *What a great day we had together. We will have to do this again.*

The Anniversary Road Trip

Ben Brecht (brother to Mary)
Jeanette (wife to Ben), Mary
Regina – June 2018

"I got something in the mail a few days ago; I keep forgetting to show you. It's over there." My mother pointed to her TV stand.

"It's an invitation to a 60th Wedding Anniversary party," I told her. I continued to read about the event for her brother, Ben, and his wife, Jeanette. "It's in Regina at the end of June."

"And I am invited?" asks Mom.

"Yes, you are invited and look at their beautiful picture, from their wedding day. What a lovely couple." I showed Mom the invitation with the picture of the couple on their wedding day. "I don't know how I would get there," she wondered out loud.

"If you would like to go, we can take you," I offered, referring to my husband and myself.

"How would we get there, where would we stay, and what about my wheelchair and walker?" she asked.

"Ma," I said, "If you want to go, I will happily take you. We will drive and stay in a hotel, and I will look after everything for you, including the packing and taking your wheelchair and your walker. And I will get you a new outfit for the anniversary."

"I have money," she started, and I cut her off, "Ma, you don't need to spend your money. We will look after that, and you don't need to worry about anything; you just need to be a Queen for the day, smile, and enjoy yourself."

"Oh, I can't be the Queen; my sister is the Queen," she retorted with a laugh.

"Of course, you can be the Queen for the day — and you will have an outfit fit for a Queen," I assured her.

"That would be wonderful; you will do that for me?" she responded, looking for confirmation.

"Of course, I will do that for you; you are my mother. I will let them know we are coming," I replied.

"Thank you for being my daughter," was her only response.

I bought her two flowered dresses to choose from. She selected the one that reminded her of Easter, with soft mauve lilies woven through other spring colours on a soft white background that graduated to a dark blue at the hem. We paired the beautiful dress with black tights and her favourite pink jacket. When she tried on the outfit, now paired with a gold and pearl necklace and a matching bracelet, she indeed looked like a Queen.

We set off early on a Saturday in late June. The morning was clear and warm, making it a good day for travel. Mom and my husband had their usual caffé mochas, and I had tea. As my husband performed the chauffeur duties, I sat in the back with Mom and we chatted and listened to her favourite old-time music.

Davidson was our midway stop. It was selected because of its wheelchair-friendly washrooms at the gas station, but the process was a challenge, nonetheless. However, with my husband's assistance, we maneuvered Mom into the bathroom and on and off the toilet, washed her hands, and got back on the road for the remainder of the journey. No doubt, this situation created anxiety for my poor husband, who was left standing inside the bathroom, with ladies coming and going, repeating the sentence, "Excuse me, ladies, I am just here helping my mother-in-law, who is in the cubicle with my wife."

Mom, as usual, expressed thanks for his help and saw the humour in him having to be in the ladies' washroom. Her standard expression of appreciation had taken the form of "Thank you for being my son-in-law." Other times, she would say to him, "Thank you for being my favourite son-in-law," accompanied by a mischievous smile.

Upon arriving in Regina, we encountered road construction near the hotel; we could see the hotel, but we could not get to it. We experienced great difficulty with Siri, our in-car navigation system which repeatedly rerouted us into the road closure area, a fact that was obvious even to my mother.

Mom voiced her observation, "We have been down this same bumpy road many times, and we never end up at the hotel. Something must be wrong with the lady on the radio." Her remarks made us all laugh, and we decided to go it alone and, without Siri's help, found our way to the hotel.

Mom commented, "I told you the radio lady didn't know how to get here." My husband and I smiled. I guess she didn't.

We could feel the warmth of the early afternoon sun and a gentle breeze as we got out of the car — a perfect day for an anniversary. As I entered the hotel lobby, pushing Mom in her wheelchair, the first people we saw were Mom's sister, Brigetta, and her husband, Bob. The two sisters were immediately overtaken with smiles, laughter, and tears of joy. They hugged and kissed one another as sisters do when they have not seen each other for a long time.

At this point, seeing the joy Mom experienced made the preparation that had gone into the trip well worth the effort. And from here, it just got better.

When we arrived in our room, there were none of Mom's usual room and bed inspections. From her many years of work at The Bessborough, any hotel she stayed at would be inspected. Unfortunately, over the past few years, she had forgotten the pleasure and pride her work had brought her, and there were no more inspections or shared comraderie with the housekeeping staff. But despite her loss of much of the past, she was extremely excited and happy to be here, in the moment, at the anniversary, even though its entirety may not be recalled later.

I tried to convince Mom to nap before dressing in her Queen's outfit for dinner and the party. She was so excited, she couldn't sleep and kept talking about how much she had missed her family. Her sister, Brigetta, called and then came to our room with her husband and other relatives for a visit with Mom. Brigetta is the baby girl of the family of eleven, the second youngest. She was one of the sisters who lived near Mom when she lived in her penthouse, and they used to see each other weekly. Since Mom had moved to Prince Albert, it was more difficult for her family to visit her. Brigetta's husband, Bob, is the brother-in-law who used to call them the "twisted sisters" in jest. At this point in their lives, the sisters were not nearly as mischievous as they used to be. Mom recognized everyone, laughed, and talked happily with them about adventures they once had and life growing up on the farm. She could not contain her pleasure.

After the collection of family left, I helped Mom dress, fixed her hair, and put on her red lipstick and rouge. "Ma, you look beautiful. You look like an elegant Queen," I said. "I'll show you in the mirror."

I pushed her wheelchair to the mirror, and she

stood up and stretched tall to see herself. "Well, I am dressed up very nicely, and my hair is good, too. Maybe I do look a bit like a Queen," she mused as she tilted her head, touched her hair and then her necklace. A bit of a smile crossed her face.

"Yes, you look just like a Queen," I affirmed. "Now, let's go to see Uncle Ben and Aunt Jeanette."

Mom was anxious to see the rest of her relatives. At ninety-five years old, she was the oldest living sibling from the family of eleven. Both of her remaining brothers were at the anniversary, but only one of her two remaining sisters, Brigetta, was present. The anniversary couple's two children, along with their partners and children, were also attending. Many of my mother's cousins were present. My husband and I were invited as my cousins knew Mom could not travel on her own. We were happy to be included.

When I wheeled Mom into the party room, the smell of fresh-cut flowers filled the air. The anniversary couple stood, arm in arm, and as guests approached, unlinked their arms to welcome guests with hugs and kisses. Mom's brother, Ben, had always stood very straight and tall, a distinguished-looking gentleman, yet open and friendly. He still presented in that manner, only a thinner, grey-haired version. Again, I felt comfort, warmth, and welcome in his presence. He was quick to flash a smile, and this time was no different, especially when he saw my Mom enter the room. More smiles, tears of joy, and hugs.

I have always admired the relationship between Ben and Jeanette, the anniversary couple. I have rarely seen a couple more devoted to one another and their family. Through the hardships and good times, they faced everything as a couple, even the diagnosis of Ben's Alzheimer's. Like my Mom, they practiced their faith daily, which gave them strength, love for one another, and a love of life. Jeanette, continued to care for Ben lovingly, even as his Alzheimer's disease advanced. She said she was blessed to be able to care for him. I admire her commitment and their enduring love.

Like my mother, her brother, Peter, was in a wheelchair. His son accompanied him. My cousin and I parked the wheelchairs together in an open area of the room. Family members came and greeted our parents with smiles and hugs. Mom, surrounded by the familiarity of family, was in heaven. She sipped her wine and reminisced with her relatives, looking to me to guide her through conversations or to remind her of the identity of the relatives who greeted her.

Brother and sister were united after being

apart for several years and were comforted by each other's presence. Like Mom, Peter was afflicted by Alzheimer's and lived in a care home.

When one of his nephews asked him, "Well, Uncle Peter, how has your day been so far?"

Standing - **Ben Brecht (brother to Mary)**
Brigetta Bondnarchuk (sister to Mary)
Sitting - **Peter Brecht (brother to Mary), Mary**
Regina – June 2018

He responded with, "I have had a very busy day. The staff got me up early and gave me breakfast and then I drove to work and supervised the new jobsite. I took off a bit early so I could come here. It is busy in construction right now."

The nephew offered, "Uncle Peter, you live in a care home now where they look after you and you don't have to go to work anymore."

This comment lit Uncle Peter up, who responded in a loud, stern, fast-talking voice, "Yes, I went to work today. I go to work every day. I live in a place where they help me and make my meals but I still go to work every day and run the business. I have ran the business over fifty years and I am not going to stop now."

No one challenged his reality after his emphatic statements.

The anniversary was a beautiful opportunity for Mom and her brothers to spend time together as they no longer could frequently or easily visit each other. Though they recognized and were pleased to see one another, it was a somewhat hollow togetherness. Alzheimer's had taken their vast knowledge and depth of character and replaced it with superficial phrases, common to each of them as they struggled to relate, even in the familiarity of their relationships as brothers and sisters. Mom's sister, Brigetta, who was present and not afflicted with Alzheimer's, gently prompted her siblings' memories, as they struggled to bring specific memories back to enjoy them with her. Mom and her brothers looked to their family for support, just as children do when unsure of what response is expected. A prompt was generally accepted and appreciated. Recall and emotions are hard work when your brain connections no longer function properly. So, this lack of awareness is masked with common phrases and responses. "I am as good as it gets," "As good as can be expected," "I think I am okay," or "I live to see another day." Mom's standard response, "So far, so good."

At dinner, we were seated with Brigetta and Bob; they have also been together for many years and have met life's challenges with grace and faith. My cousins, Debra, Russ, and Amby also shared our table. By this time, there were signs that Mom was both physically and emotionally tired. Sitting low and still in her wheelchair with a blanket around her torso and legs, she could not recall the names of some of the family members at the table and asked me several times who these people were. A few hours earlier, she knew their names. She was repeating the same stories about us not being able to find the hotel and about a time at a family reunion, many years ago, when the whole family was together. The family sitting around the table were very gracious, listening to her and offering words when hers would not come.

I asked her if she wanted to rest briefly before the evening activity started, and she refused. She didn't want to miss anything.

The old-fashioned tinkling of glasses during dinner was intended to have the bride and the groom kiss. When the tinkling began, Uncle Ben stood up, rubbed his hands together, and said, "Oh, goody." He kissed his bride of sixty years with the love and passion of a newlywed. What a joyful moment for them and the family who witnessed this special kiss, a heartwarming testament to their love.

The partner of the anniversary couple's granddaughter made cakes that were marvelous pieces of art. Uncle Ben and Aunt Jeannette loved to travel, and the cakes represented that love. They were shaped like actual suitcases stacked on top of one another with stickers of all the places they had been.

After the cake presentation, a video of the life of my aunt and uncle was played. Uncle Ben watched with awe as he saw himself, his wife, family, and friends engaged in events over their shared life. It was heartwarming, touching, and humorous as the family smiled, laughed out loud, and touched their hands to their chests as they watched and listened. During the presentations, the anniversary couple sat cuddled, their hands gently clasped, smiles on their faces, and tears in their eyes. At times, they burst into laughter at the pictures of their past. Sometimes, Uncle Ben shared puzzled looks with his bride of sixty years. Aunt Jeanette reassured him that the images of the man in the video were of him; he smiled, nodded, and continued holding her hand.

After the video and cutting of the cakes, Uncle Ben's son toasted them, and offered wishes for many more years of happiness together — such fitting tributes to a couple who embodied life together in a loving marriage of sixty years. Their hearts were warm and full, even though Uncle Ben did not recall the full details of his life or their life together. He, too, was happy in the moment.

The evening continued with more visiting and reminiscing, old-time music playing in the background. The family was together, celebrating a lifetime of love. They felt blessed to be sharing this occasion. My mom said she felt blessed to be with her family.

As I helped Mom remove her Queen outfit, I knew she was exhausted. She said she had to "sleep fast," which she always said when she was very tired and needed to go to bed immediately. Within minutes of tucking her in, I could hear her peaceful snoring. I am sure her senses were overwhelmed by all the emotions and activities of the day.

The next morning, Mom was refreshed, clear-minded and eager to eat breakfast with Brigetta,

Bob, and her cousin. We shared our views of how perfect the anniversary was as we enjoyed our food. We talked about how it makes one's heart feel so full to be with one another again. When Mom was teased about some incidents from her past, she smiled and laughed about those good times. She did not recall all the details her family were telling her. Nevertheless, she was happy to be in the company of her family.

There were more hugs and tears of joy and sadness as Mom said goodbye. Her heart was fully recharged from spending time with her family. She was tired out, but it was a good tired.

On the way home, I sat in the back seat again with Mom. Her old-time music was playing. We talked occasionally, but she slept most of the way home. We stopped at the same washroom in Davidson and my husband helped me with Mom in the ladies' washroom one more time. Fortunately, there were no ladies in the bathroom for him to apologize to this time. With her sense of humour, Mom recognized that and grinned, saying to my husband, "Thank you for being my son-in-law and not scaring the other ladies this time."

Mom was eager to get back to her room at her care home. Before resting, she shared all the details she could recall about her trip and the anniversary with the staff. As I put her things away, I heard her emphatically tell the staff, "My favourite part of the trip was spending time with my family again; my heart is full of love again. I am happy I got to go."

As I kissed her goodbye, she said, "Thank you for taking me and thank you for being my daughter. I love you."

I replied, "Thank you for being my mother. I love you too."

This would be the last big road trip I had the pleasure of taking my mom on. Reflecting on it, I am grateful for the honour and the opportunity to bring happiness to Mom's heart on that special anniversary occasion.

An Angel for Mary

Wanlta (outside in the cold)
Mary (inside the building)
Wanda (outside in the cold)
fighting COVID restrictions
Winter 2020

Mom believed that angels were sent to protect us, intervene on our behalf, and guide us through life's daily challenges. She found strength in praying to angels, faithfully reading her Bible, and holding her angel cards to connect with the energies of angels. Sometimes, she said, angels were real people who appeared in certain situations, and sometimes, they were divine intervention from Heaven.

Mom said that her mother-in-law often talked about having angels help her. There was the time when she prayed for one of her nieces to find a good Hungarian husband and, lo and behold, one appeared, the work of an angel and divine intervention according to her. She said "Thanks be to God" many times in a day for the little pleasures and the good things she experienced.

Like her mother-in-law's life, my mother's was filled with prayers to both angels and saints.

As a woman of faith, Mom prayed for guidance and strength and shared her wisdom with her family and others. She believed in praying to saints for certain things. For example, if you lost something and could not find it, you would pray to St. Anthony. I would tell her about a particular problem, and Mom would tell me to pray to a saint for guidance. I would pray and report to Mom that my prayer had no positive result.

"Which saint did you pray to?" she would ask.

"I didn't know there were specific saints for each issue. I should just be able to pray, and my prayer should get to the saint who could look after the problem for me."

"It doesn't work like that; you have to pray to the saint that looks after that area."

In frustration, I would grumble, "Then you pray to the right saint for me!"

Mom would agree to pray to the saint for me and soon after her prayers, a solution to my problem would present itself.

The family would often tease Mom that she had a special connection to the Lord and that the Lord was always by her side. For example, when she played cards, her friendly competitors would say the Lord was playing with her; when they played the card game, Golf, and she turned her cards over, miraculously, they would match and she would win. Mom would smile and laugh. Lucky or the work of the Lord?

Mom and her family believed it to be the work of the Lord, a belief that was verified when Mom had her brain bleed in 2013 and was on death's door. She prayed for more years with her family, and the Lord granted her many more.

Mom was ninety-two years old when Leslie appeared in her life. Leslie was a self-assured, confident, woman with curly, short, red hair and a sparsely-freckled face. She was a community-minded, caring woman, an artist, and a curler who, just before retiring from a successful career in design, decided to take up massage therapy. Leslie had lost her elderly parents a few years prior and, inspired to give back to the elderly community, began to do foot massages to comfort the elderly in care homes. At Wanda's request, I arranged for Leslie to meet Mom to see if they would get along well as a client and therapist.

Leslie and Mary had many things in common. They were both women of faith and prayer. They had a positive outlook, were grateful for what they had, and accepted change as a cycle of life. Each embraced a new day and gracefully accepted the joy and blessings it would bring. Both were active and healthy, had had successful work careers, and had pride in completing tasks to a high level of satisfaction. Mary had had a very active life — working full-time, being a family bread winner, and being a mother. Leslie admired what Mom had accomplished in her lifetime and that she was such a strong independent woman. Mary was an inspiration and a hero to Leslie.

Leslie and Mom's first visit to see if they would be a good match was comparable to when Mom first met her new doctor a few years earlier. When Mom was introduced to the woman who might be her new doctor, she asked, "So, are you going to be my new doctor?"

The doctor replied, "Would it be all right with you if I were your doctor?"

Mom responded, "I think that will be okay."

Mom's conversation with Leslie, the potential foot massage lady, was similar. Mom asked, "So, are you going to be my foot massage lady?"

Leslie replied, "Yes, I could be, if it is all right with you."

"Yes, I think that will be fine; I think we will get along okay," Mom responded.

As they continued chatting during the first foot massage, they agreed that they were a good fit for each other and that Leslie would be "the foot massage lady," as Mom called her.

Leslie and Mom both looked forward to the foot massage sessions. Mom often did not remember Leslie's name, but she knew her face and liked to talk to Leslie while enjoying her foot massage. These times lifted Mom's spirits. Leslie appreciated the opportunity to help improve Mom's health and mood and felt heartened and soothed by their chats. Their relationship deepened as they talked and shared stories about their work, families, and experiences in life.

Leslie knew that Mom had Alzheimer's so every

massage would begin the same. "Hi Mary, it's Leslie; I am here to massage your feet again. You look lovely today, as usual. How was your day?" Leslie would say, as she put on Mom's music and fetched the stool from the closet to rest Mary's feet on during the massage. "You can tell me if there is anything you need help with today while I massage."

"Oh, I thought I knew you! You are the foot massage lady. It feels good when you massage my feet," Mom would respond. And Mom would tell Leslie how her day had gone and anything that may be significant to her — as much as Mom could remember!

Mom sat in her light green wingback chair that once had graced the Bessborough Hotel. Like Mom, it had aged with grace. Leslie would raise one of Mom's feet and place it on a towel on the footstool. When Leslie placed her foot on the stool, Mom would tell her that her father had made the stool many years ago. They would continue to talk while Leslie massaged her feet. Leslie had realized that Mom loved to pray and listen to her old-time music so she would put the music on softly so that Mom could hear it and chat simultaneously. Other times, Mom would read her prayers aloud to Leslie. The more Leslie learned about Mom's life, family, and activities, the more she came to admire Mom as an accepting, humble, loving woman of faith, strength, resilience, and courage.

Before Leslie retired she often arranged to do Mom's foot massage on her way from work and before Mom had supper. The schedule changed once Leslie retired but she still liked to massage Mom's feet before supper. Leslie would be nearly finished the treatment when a staff member would come and announce that supper would be served shortly. The care worker would continue down the hall, alerting each resident that they should proceed to the dining room. Then the staff person would return to help those, like Mom, who required support and supervision to attend the dining room. By dinner time, Leslie had finished Mom's foot massage, found her ever-elusive rosary, and arranged her prayer books. The care staff would assist Mom to the bathroom, where she would wash up and renew her fading red lipstick. Then they would walk to the dining room, the staff person on one side of Mom, who would walk with her walker, and Leslie on the other. Often, Mom would ask, "What do I do now?"

The care staff and Leslie would respond in unison, "Supper is starting in the dining room now, Mary. We are taking you there."

Mom would politely smile, nod, and respond, "Thank you. I can always eat."

Once Mom was seated in the dining room, Leslie would chat with her and the other ladies at the table until supper was served. At that point, she would hug Mom and be on her way.

After visiting Mom, Leslie often called me to ask about a particular story Mom had told her. This gave Leslie a greater understanding of Mom's remembrance, which may differ from what had actually occurred at the time. Leslie would also pass on information about how Mom was doing and any issues that Mom brought up that she thought should be addressed. These conversations gave me more perspective about Mom and her well-being.

In one such call, Leslie reported that Mom was very distressed as her sister had not returned a suitcase that she had borrowed. She said she needed the things in the suitcase and that it was in the storage area at the top of the barn at the family farm. Leslie indicated this was not the first time Mom had mentioned the misplaced suitcase. This time, though, Mom had become very emotionally unsettled when she told Leslie about the missing suitcase and its contents. I told Leslie that Mom had mentioned this missing piece of luggage several times over the past year, but now due to Mom's increasing distress regarding the suitcase, I set out to solve the mystery.

I found out that Mom attended a family wedding

along with her sister Winnie, her other siblings, and in-laws. Mom's brothers and brothers-in-law were practical jokers. When they went to pick up Mom's sister, Winnie, they teased her that she did not need a suitcase and that they would not bring it. Neither of her brothers put the bag in the van, not out of mischief but because each thought the other had put it in the van. In all their joking, they had accidentally left it behind. It was only when they arrived to pick Mom up and set her suitcase in the van, did they realize that Winnie's suitcase was not there.

Mom lent Winnie a suitcase, some clothes, and personal care items, and off they went to the wedding. The brothers and brothers-in-law thought this was so funny. Mom's sister did not believe it was amusing at the time, but saw the humour in the situation over time. Nevertheless, she said that Mom saved the day.

This was the "missing" suitcase Mom referred to. However, it was certainly long gone and no longer returnable. After many discussions with Mom, Leslie and I relieved Mom of her worry over the suitcase and convinced her that the items were no longer useful to her. Mom was finally satisfied, at peace, and could let go.

One Christmas, Leslie came to the rescue when I could not attend the Christmas party at Mom's personal care home. Mom loved Christmas and all the activities and was looking forward to the annual Christmas event. Most of the residents had family or a friend attending and Mom was downhearted that none of her family could attend the Christmas party with her. Leslie knew this and offered to be her escort for the celebration.

When Leslie arrived, she saw Mom seated at a table, smartly dressed in her new red festive outfit, with her grey hair perfectly combed, and her red lipstick and nail polish flawlessly applied. The bewildered look on Mom's face did not match her outfit or the setting. As Leslie approached, Mom heaved a sigh of relief and waved at Leslie with a forced smile. Once Leslie was seated beside her, she sighed again deeply, her forced expression relaxing into a genuine smile. Now, it would be a joyous afternoon. Leslie was here!

The dining room was decorated with red bells, bows, mistletoe, and streamers of green garland. The vaulted ceiling hosted a ten-foot-tall evergreen tree decorated with sparkling lights, colourful glass balls, and decorations handmade by the residents. The tables were set with printed cloths fitting the Christmas season, festive glass Christmas dishes, and red and green fabric napkins embossed with the words *Merry Christmas*. A special chair in the middle of all the Christmas tables was decorated with bells and bows for Santa.

The lunch was plentiful and delicious, with shrimp, hors d'oeuvres, dips, cheese, fruit, and dainty desserts. The residents and their guests enjoyed lunch and a glass of wine together, sang Christmas carols, and visited. When Santa arrived, he cheerfully hugged and chatted with each of the residents as he presented them a gift. It was a beautiful Christmas celebration! Mom and Leslie felt blessed to spend the time together enjoying the spirit of Christmas.

In appreciation for Leslie coming to the Christmas party, Mom gifted Leslie with a box of chocolates and Christmas card picture of herself. Leslie treasured the picture. Every Christmas, Mom would give Leslie a new Christmas card picture of herself and Leslie would place it inside the front cover of her daily affirmation book.

At times, when I had to be out of town for work, and Mom had no one to visit her, Leslie would volunteer to check on Mom and massage her feet while there. Leslie would then report to me how Mom was doing and if she had any issues that needed my attention. Leslie would happily join in on other special occasions at the care home, like Mother's Day Tea or birthday parties. Leslie was like family.

COURAGE AND A CASTLE

During COVID-19, personal care homes did not allow visitors inside for health and safety reasons. Like all others, our family visited Mom through the glass door; she inside the building, and the family members outside. Even though my sisters and I were pleased to physically see our mother and better understand how she was doing during this time of isolation, everyone, especially Mom, found this physical barrier challenging to adjust to.

Once vaccination took place, residents were sometimes allowed to use personal care services. That is where Leslie, like an angel, intervened again. As she offered a personal care service, foot massage, she was allowed to attend Mom's room. During COVID-19, she would weekly bring cheer and hope to Mom. She massaged Mom's feet during the visits and assisted her with any little tasks that she needed help with, such as getting her a snack and a cup of tea, finding her rosary and prayer book, setting up the word game on her tablet, and playing her old-time music. I was grateful to have first-hand information about Mom's well-being from Leslie. After talking with Leslie, I would speak with care home staff to ensure Mom's needs were addressed. This worked well during the time I was not allowed to go in for visits.

Alzheimer's had overtaken Mom's ability to recall most daily activities and describe her feelings;

COVID-19 restrictions, isolation and non-contact took an additional toll. Over time, restrictions were lifted briefly, but then reinstated. Mom grew tired quickly of the visits through glass doors, but it was one of the only two ways to see her family. The other was through video calls using her tablet, a process which was also exceedingly difficult for her as she often pressed the wrong buttons on the tablet and accidentally ended the call. So, the family was left with telephone calls that required clarification regarding Mom's well-being because her memory was not very reliable due to her Alzheimer's. However, as Leslie provided personal care services, she was again allowed into the care home to massage Mom's feet. Leslie's physical presence in Mom's room and genuine emotional connection lifted Mom's spirits and gave her hope for a better tomorrow. What a blessing!

On the first COVID-19 Christmas in 2020, due to the restrictions, there would be no gatherings or celebrations in the care home or anywhere else.

Knowing Mom's love of the holiday, Leslie offered to take in a small Christmas tree and decorate it as well as Mom's room. While decorating, Leslie played Christmas music and they both sang and hummed along to "Little Drummer Boy." Leslie then repeated one of Mom's favourite daily prayers with Mom while she massaged her feet. On a subsequent visit, Leslie brought Christmas presents from Mom's family. Leslie set up and monitored the video call so my sisters could watch and interact with Mom as she opened her Christmas gifts with Leslie's assistance. My sisters were so delighted they could see and visit Mom at Christmas through Leslie. More blessings!

Mary's Christmas Tree
December 2020

Although that would be Mom's last Christmas, it was one she enjoyed with a Christmas tree, decorated room, Christmas music, Christmas gifts, and prayer. On Christmas Day, the residents were treated to a delicious turkey dinner, a favorite meal of Mom's.

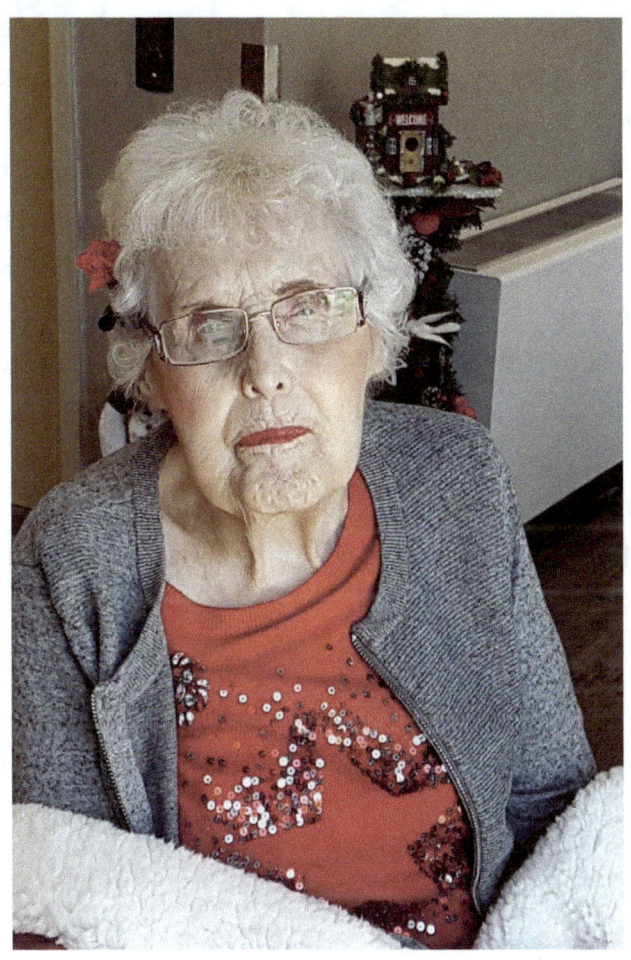

Mary
COVID quarantine
Christmas 2020

Despite the circumstances, Mom embraced the spirit of Christmas as much as possible. But, of course, she did; she had angelic intervention! Mom and my sisters were blessed to share Mom's last Christmas with her while she was in the company of her Angel Leslie, who also cared deeply for Mom.

The role of angels is to provide protection, intervention, guidance, and comfort and to nurture each of us to meet our daily challenges. Sometimes, they assist and guide us in ways we are unaware of; other times, our angels are real people given to us in our daily lives. For Mom, Leslie was her real-life angel!

Leslie keeps the last Christmas card picture of Mom in her daily affirmation journal. She greets each day with joy and gratitude as she recites her affirmation and gazes affectionately at the picture of Mom who is still a woman of strength and an inspiration for her.

Hospital

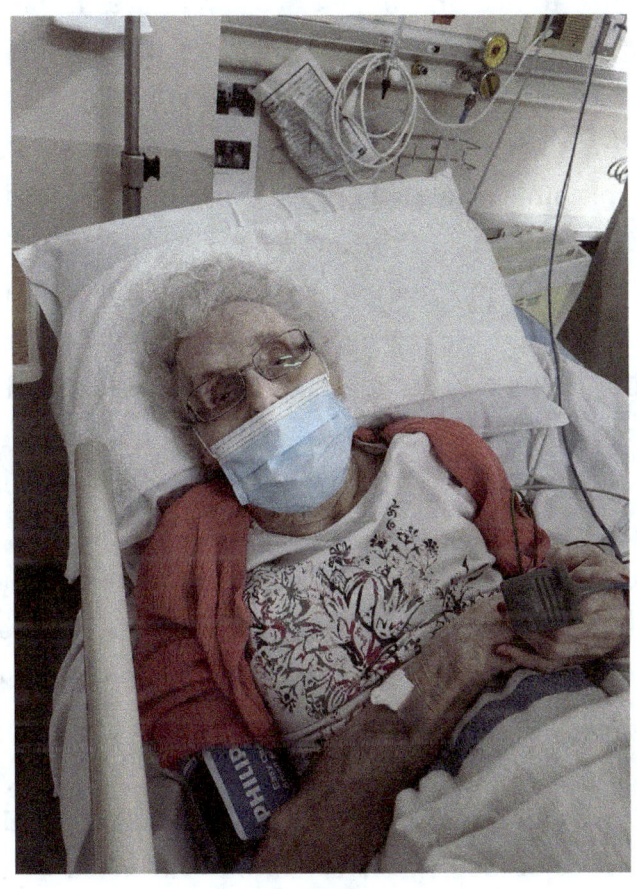

Mary
Prince Albert Hospital
April 2021

In early April 2021, concerned care home staff called me to tell me Mom, bemoaning that she was tired, refused to get out of bed for lunch. Earlier that morning, she had gotten out of bed but then had only picked at her breakfast before she immediately returned to bed and pulled her covers over her head. This behaviour was out of character for Mom.

It was the height of COVID-19. Vaccinations had just begun. Masking was mandatory, visitors were prohibited, and there were even restrictions on residents' movement inside the facility.

The staff put me on speakerphone and, after much pleading on my part, Mom reluctantly agreed to uncover her head so we could talk. I was finally able to convince her to go to the dining room and at least have a snack and tea. After that, she could take a nap. I explained that she needed to be a bit more mobile as we did not want her to be moved to a long-term care facility during COVID-19. Finally, and begrudgingly, Mom agreed to sit up, let the staff put her shoes on, take her to the bathroom, and then to the dining room in her wheelchair.

Occasionally, over the past few months, Mom mentioned that she had double vision for short periods of time. In the past few weeks, Mom had more days when she was tired, which was uncommon, but she always made an effort to get out of bed and move about with staff assistance. I worried that if she became less mobile, she would be sent to long-term care. With COVID-19 restrictions, I would not be able to facilitate her orientation to a new care home. As well, there were more COVID-19 containment issues in long-term care homes and less interaction with staff; Mom's pleasant but restricted daily life would have been totally disrupted in unfamiliar surroundings with caregivers and residents she did not know.

The inactivity, lack of contact with family and the long winter had taken a toll on Mom and others in care homes. At that time, residents were confined to their rooms, but after the "not getting out of bed" incident, I contacted the care home owner and pleaded with her that I be allowed to come in and see Mom.

I talked with Mom's doctor and requested that she write me a letter stating that my mom needed my assistance as her health was deteriorating. The doctor indicated that she did not have authority over the Health Region's directive regarding visitors.

Again, I approached the care home owner, and she finally agreed that I could come in a few times and sit with Mom, but only in her room. (At that time, residents were confined to their rooms.) We decided I could come for lunch, stay the afternoon and, over supper, help her eat, and keep her company. The staff would bring lunch and supper meals to her room for both of us. I was relieved I could spend time with Mom during this time of isolation and fear.

One of the things Mom often said was, "I can always eat." Well, not anymore. No matter what was served, and they made special mushy food she liked, such as mashed potatoes, gravy, and butterscotch pudding, she would nibble only a few bites before saying, "I can't eat anymore."

I would offer to feed her, but she would choose to eat on her own, and then only pick at the food offered. With a bit of coaching, she would eat a few more bites. After lunch, we would call family she had not spoken with for some time. They were thrilled to talk to Mom. The staff and I would then take her to the bathroom and tuck her into bed. She looked forward to being covered up to her chin and nestled safely under her warm blanket, her music playing low in the background.

I was genuinely concerned about her declining health. In this past year, since I last was able to visit with her face-to-face, she had significantly aged. She had gotten smaller and seemed less enthusiastic towards each new day. Damn COVID-19! How could I help Mom if I couldn't be there with her?

After a nap, it was time for tea, and we would

sit side by side, play her Find-a-Word puzzles on her tablet, and listen to her waltzes and polkas. Sometimes, we would play Bingo via video with family members. She was always quick to call "Bingo!" Other times, phone or video calls with family members included general chit-chat and prayers.

I would place her rosary on her pillow and her prayer binder on her bed for easy access. A favourite prayer, "Walk In The World For Me" was the last prayer in her prayer binder. A copy of the prayer was also on the table beside her high back, queen-like, Bessborough chair. Mom still liked to pray, though sometimes she would now skip some pages in her prayer binder; when she was feeling better she would repeat her prayers several times a day.

Visits by non-personal-care professionals were still restricted and in the middle of the second week of my visits, I was advised by the care home owner that I could no longer come in; people had complained that she was allowing me to visit. I was devastated, and Mom didn't understand why I didn't come and see her anymore. I explained to Mom that I wanted to come and see her daily but I was not allowed to. She didn't fully understand and when she talked to my sisters, she would tell them I didn't come to see her anymore, and she didn't know why. They would refresh her memory as to the COVID-19 rules.

Monday (April 26, 2021)

I got a call that Mom had been taken by ambulance to the hospital. I had not seen her for a week. The owner of the care home reported that Mom, who was ninety-seven-years-old at that time, had fallen while walking out of her room into the hallway. She told me she did not know if anything was broken, but that Mom had been behaving oddly that morning. She told me Mom was taken to the hospital by ambulance. I thanked her for the prompt report, and I was on my way, making the twenty-five minute drive in twenty minutes.

As I drove, I hoped this was nothing significant and she would not have to be hospitalized for broken bones.

When I found Mom in an examination room in the emergency area, she was jittery, anxious and alone. Her tiny figure took up little space on the gurney. Her pink sweater hung open, revealing her floral and white top. She was covered from the waist down with a flannel blanket. Though she had the required mask on her face, it was tucked under her chin as if she found breathing through it difficult. When she saw me, her lips unsuccessfully tried to turn upwards to form a smile, and her fingers waved nervously for me to come closer.

We were immensely relieved to see one another. The fear in her eyes dissipated momentarily as we put our arms around one another and drew each other near. I could feel her tense body relax as we hugged.

The hospital staff had started an intravenous drip and were conducting tests. Mom was little Miss Chatterbox, but unfortunately much of her chatter seemed out of context and I had difficulty following the threads of the information she eagerly shared. She was aware she was in the hospital and said her bum hurt. She asked me how I learned she was in the hospital and then told me what she recalled about her fall.

She said that her dad was sitting on the sofa in the living room just off the dining room at the care home. While she nibbled her breakfast, he talked to her, informing her that he was waiting for her to accompany him. When she was ready to return to her room, he was gone. Shortly after lunch, a boy she did not know entered her room. She was trying to chase him out when she fell.

She didn't remember that she needed to use her walker and had shuffled through the doorway into the hall without it. It was there that she fell, but was fortunately found immediately by the staff. Later, the staff told me that she told them the same story about her father and the little boy, but neither her father nor a boy had been seen by anyone but Mother.

The doctor arrived and shared information

about Mom's condition. Her heart rate was 38 beats per minute when she was admitted, more than 20 bpm lower than normal. She had a third-degree heart block, which meant a complete loss of communication between the atria and the ventricles, resulting in her heart not pumping enough blood to her brain and body, which is why she was tired and wanted to sleep. He said, essentially, her heart was worn out.

An involuntary laugh escaped from my throat. How could this be? Even though Alzheimer's affected her, she was still a healthy and vibrant woman. This news took me by surprise but it did explain her recent behaviours. The doctor further explained that he thought there were no broken bones but would have a CT scan done to rule out any possible breaks. He also ordered a test to rule out a bladder infection. Mom was susceptible to bladder infections and, in the past few years, did not recognize the physical symptoms. So when she was extra tired, had difficulty going to the bathroom, and was more forgetful and confused than usual, we would have her tested for bladder infection. Most times, that was the problem and antibiotics would have her feeling better in no time. The doctor ended his update by telling us that he would speak to us again after the tests were complete.

Mid-evening, Mom was moved to a cubicle

in the emergency room. There were curtains on three sides, and patients with various conditions occupied the beds around her cubicle. As I was vaccinated, I was allowed to stay with her as long as I wore a gown and a mask. Everyone was required to wear a mask. This included Mom, who continued to pull hers off. As she was uncomfortable and could not comprehend its need, I did not replace it.

Mom was stressed and tried to rest but couldn't stop talking. She lifted herself to a sitting position by pulling on the handrails of the hospital bed. She told me that she needed to get out of bed because she had work to do. She had been preparing food all day and needed to get up and peel the potatoes. She cleaned the house, baked bread, and made cabbage rolls, cake, and carrots. I volunteered to get the potatoes, peel them for her and mash them once they were cooked. She slumped back onto the bed and thanked me, then repeatedly asked if I would make the potatoes for her. Although I asked, she had no idea where we were, what year we were in, what event she was preparing for, or who was coming ... "They are all coming," she assured me.

Mom was exhausted from all her "work," the trauma of her fall, and her faintly beating heart. I encouraged her to rest. As we talked, a nurse entered the cubicle and inserted a catheter as Mom was too weak to get out of bed. A few minutes after she left, the curtain swiftly swung open, and two nurses burst in to check on Mom. She had a heart monitor on, and the computer at the nursing desk indicated Mom had an extremely fast heartbeat. The nurses thought she might be having a heart attack, thus their haste in entering the cubicle.

Meanwhile, as the nurses rushed in, I saw Mom tapping her fingers rapidly on her chest close to the heart monitoring device. My anxious Mother had no idea what the fuss was about and smiled innocently as the nurses and I tried to explain why she should stop the tapping motion. Repetitive motions, purposeful breathing, humming, and music help calm the nervous system and reduce stress. Mom intuitively knew this and practiced it all her life. However, her gentle, continuous tapping by the heart monitoring device created stress for the rest of us at this particular time. After Mom understood what had happened, she finally settled on humming, which comforted her. However, that was frequently interrupted by her sharing of incomprehensible bits of information about a family gathering and a host of other thoughts I could not connect.

I had been communicating with my sisters, brother and other family members about Mom's condition while I sat with her. Sometimes, Mom talked with them on video phone, and other times,

I stepped out of her area. Just before midnight, the doctor returned to confirm that Mom had no broken bones and no bladder infection. It was simply the worn-out condition of her heart. He explained the options and then facilitated a video call with my sisters to review the diagnosis and discuss options for us to decide on a course of action. The doctor told us that with her heart condition, she could live a few days, a few weeks, or a few months.

Our family was shaken and stunned by this news. However, we agreed that Mom should not have a pacemaker to manage her diagnosis of third-degree heart blockage. There was risk and further trauma to have a pacemaker implanted and no promise of increased quality of life or life span. We were also advised that Mom would require more care than could be given at her current personal care home, so she must go into a long-term care facility when she was released. My sisters and I were emotionally exhausted, as was Mom, from all the trauma the day had brought, but we were satisfied Mom was receiving good care in the hospital, and she would rebound and get better, as she always did.

Mom was kept overnight for observation and stabilization and given a sleeping pill to calm her and help her relax and rest. Her mostly indecipherable, nonstop dialogue continued, despite her fatigue. None of my soothing words, prayers, humour, or gentle stroking of her hands and head served to quieten her. Finally, the sleeping pill settled her. I gently kissed her on the forehead and brushed her now quiet lips with my fingertips as I told her I would return in the afternoon, as the nurses had advised me that I was not allowed to stay overnight. I left to go home. It was 3:30 a.m.

Tuesday

Mom was withdrawn when I arrived in the afternoon and only responded if she was spoken to. She did not initiate conversation, nor did she interact much with the hospital staff or me. She laid, mostly still, on the hospital bed covered with only one sheet. She liked to be warm and often called herself a "freeze cat," so I covered her with more sheets and tucked them around her tightly. I kissed her on the forehead and told her I loved her, and gently stroked her worn face.

Mom looked tired and weary, her face tight with anxiety and her eyes clamped closed. She looked like she was trying hard to rest, but she did not look restful, only fretful. Her mouth was partially open, and her breathing was laboured. Sometimes she took deep inhalations as if to gather enough breath. From time to time, she cried out and moaned as if in pain. Though it has been determined that she had no broken bones, the fall had certainly brought on aches and pain.

The nurse raised Mom's bed and gave her crushed Tylenol. She fed Mom a few spoons of soup, but that was all Mom would eat. She did agree to sip a bit of Boost™. The nurse and I talked with Mom as she ate, but Mom barely spoke; she made motions and moved her head to the side when she did not want anything more to eat. She was given jelly-like water so as not to choke while swallowing. Her bed was lowered, her pillow adjusted, and her blankets were tucked around her as she attempted to "sleep fast." Unfortunately, at this time, her discomfort did not allow her peaceful sleep.

While I sat with Mom, I kept our family apprised of her condition. She talked with them briefly on the phone and listened to my brother's prayers. Her body relaxed as he prayed.

My sisters from out of province planned to come and spend time with Mom and she was looking forward to seeing them. I told Mom that she had to stay in the hospital a few more days. She replied that she wanted to come and stay with me at the acreage. I told her that could not happen right now, she needed to get a bit better first. Again, I was not allowed to stay overnight with Mom so I went home for the night.

Wednesday

I was allowed to visit again but could not stay past 8 p.m. I returned early in the morning as I was invited to attend rounds with the doctor and hospital staff to discuss Mom's condition and care. I was pleased yet apprehensive to participate. Before rounds, the nurses told me Mom had a fitful night, occasionally crying out in pain and taking only jellied water. My heart ached that Mom was suffering, and I could do nothing to relieve it.

During rounds, the doctor told me Mom had complained of pain in her tummy. They would give her an IV with fluids for her dehydration and administer pain medication through the IV. Antibiotics would also be administered, which might perk her up. The doctor briefly mentioned palliative care, saying that a designation of palliative offered more care options. I could not understand or put all the bits of information together quickly due to my own lack of sleep. I was unfamiliar with what a recommendation for palliative care fully meant, but the doctor told me it would be helpful in further planning for Mom's situation. I agreed and the doctor designated Mom palliative care.

On this day, Mom was more interactive, but her speech was laboured and brief. She was not eating or drinking; she took only the jellied water. When the nurses came to wash her and change her gown and sheets, she winced and flattened herself more firmly on the bed, and in an irritable voice said she did not want to move as it hurt to do so. The nurses were gentle and used warm water to wash her face, body, and hair. They dried and quickly covered her cleaned body so she did not get cold. They combed her hair as best they could, given that it was frazzled — just like Mom was from the trauma she was experiencing. Once she was refreshed and finished her nap, I facilitated video or telephone calls with family. They all said prayers with her and for her. That seemed to comfort her. I was hopeful, as Mom remained in good spirits, yet I was anxious about the sudden failing of her health.

Thursday

When I arrived, the nurses told me Mom's night was more peaceful and that she was now on oxygen for comfort and ease of breathing, as her oxygen levels were below 80. This, along with the antibiotics they are giving intravenously, had perked her up, and she was awake and sometimes communicating. Unfortunately, the chatty Mother from Monday was nowhere to be found. She must have used up all her words and energy that day. I tried to recall some of the comments she had made that day, but she had talked so much that my recall was blurred. However,

I was delighted she was speaking again, even if only infrequently.

Mom and I were left to ourselves while the nurses attended other patients. She was communicating with me using short sentences. I was happy to have Mom back again. When the nurses returned, they changed her gown and sheets, and gently bathed her. She liked the warmth of the wet cloth but shivered as they hurried to cover her freshly washed body. She took only partial spoons of jellied water. She was tucked in for a nap, and seemed to rest.

When she awoke, I was dismayed to note an emptiness in her eyes, as if part of her was missing or disengaged. I had not seen this before. I tried not to dwell on it, but the image replayed in my mind.

I had contacted the priest for the "last rites" to be administered to Mom and had arranged for my sisters and brother to be on video with us while the prayers were said. I had brought her a rosary and one of her well-used prayer books. They had always been significant for her in her life of hope and faith. I placed the rosary in her cold, now feeble hands and folded her wrought fingers around it. She understood what the object was and grasped it tightly. The Father spoke with Mom and stroked her messy grey hair. He accommodated my lack of knowledge of technological devices and set up his phone with a video call to my brother as I set up my tablet with my sisters. The Father began the prayers with the "Our Father," followed by the "Hail Mary," one of Mom's favourites. Wayne requested Psalm 23, "The Lord is My Shepherd," and he and the Father prayed earnestly together. Wayne routinely prayed that psalm and other prayers with Mom.

The Father ended the blessing with a last rites prayer: "Lord Jesus, holy and compassionate: forgive Mary her sins. By dying, you unlocked the gates of life for those who believe in you: do not let our sister be parted from you, but by your glorious power give her light, joy, and peace in heaven where you live and reign forever and ever. Amen."

Mom was awake with her eyes closed as the prayers were said. Her lips moved slightly as if she were praying along. She was aware of the significance of this last rite. The Father anointed her forehead and offered another blessing. Mom acknowledged his presence by gently squeezing his hand.

When I talked with the Father after he administered the last rites, I shared with him that we were raised as Catholics but went to a public school because the Catholic schools were too far away to walk to. We all took catechism lessons, were baptized, and had communion and confirmation, which were special religious family events. Attending mass on Sundays was part of our upbringing. Mom's belief in God shaped her life and ours. I told him that my father did not participate, but was supportive, insisting that we were taught Catholic values and attended church.

I shared with him that Mom believed that many angels and saints protected and guided her throughout her life and her perspective was one of gratitude, that life presented joy to be embraced. I explained that Mom modelled her beliefs and that her faith brought balance to her life — especially through the praying of the Rosary. Her father taught their family how to pray the Rosary, and she taught us how to pray the Rosary. We smiled as Mom was clutching her Rosary tightly in her hands as we were speaking. Mom and I were grateful for his comforting presence. I spent the afternoon with Mom, who was more responsive when awake and rested more peacefully with the supplemental oxygen.

In the early evening, Mom was moved to a private room. Just before the move, a nursing staff gave me a pamphlet called *"Preparing for Approaching Death."* Even though Mom had been given the "last rites," I was disturbed and uncomfortable being presented with such information. She had always recovered from whatever challenge she faced and she was *only* ninety-seven. Mom dying had not occurred to me until the pamphlet was given to me. Surely Mom was not going to die?

The staff advised me that I could stay overnight with Mom. I was so excited, but I had to wait until Mom awoke to cheerfully tell her, "Guess what, Ma, the doctor said I can sleep over with you."

She replied, "I want to come to your house to sleep over."

"Sorry, Ma, that is the best I can do today." As she was unable to sit up by herself, I showed her a picture of the chair I would sleep in and a photo of her in her hospital bed. "We will be together in the same room. I will be right there," I said, pointing to the chair and teasing her that she got the better sleeping accommodation.

"Maybe if I move over, you can sleep in my bed with me?" my ever-considerate mother wondered.

"That's okay Ma, I get to stay with you, and I will be just fine in the chair. It reclines."

The staff again gave her antibiotics in her IV, and Mom became more alert and responsive. We engaged in video and telephone conversations with family. Mom was happy to be speaking with her family and to know that her other two daughters were coming to visit. I played her favourite music from her playlist on my tablet. I found her singing along softly or humming to some of the songs as the tunes took turns wrapping Mom in the comfort of their words and familiar melodies. As songs cycled through, I noted she hummed along to "Somewhere My Love," a song I know she associated with Dad.

I was grateful I was allowed to stay with Mom overnight. She seemed to appreciate that we could sleep in the same room, even if I had to sleep in the chair. I slept in brief naps, waking whenever Mom stirred. She had a bit of a bumpy night; when she moaned with pain, the nurse promptly administered pain medication through her IV, which promoted a more restful state. She awoke occasionally and called out to check if I was still there. I would go to her bedside, kiss her on her cheek, assure her I was there, and hold her hand until sleep overtook her.

As I sat with Mom and slept in short naps, a host of emotions flowed through me, but primarily extreme sadness and fear, the fear of losing Mom. Random and impactful thoughts and memories flooded my mind, such as how, despite Mom's limited education, she sought employment and worked hard, with Dad and then on her own, to look after our family's financial needs. I admired her courage and foresight to plan for her family's growth and best interests. To this day, we children attest that her buying the Avenue T North house and moving our family was the best thing Mom ever did for us — her intuition and forward-thinking opened opportunities we would never have had if we had not moved.

For me, Mom was the foundation of our family.

She inspired me. I had no idea how I could face life without her.

Friday

I attended the daily rounds in the morning. The doctor, a nurse, and the pharmacist had discussions regarding medications for comfort measures and antibiotics for bladder infection, which they thought she might now have developed. The social worker identified that long-term care would be required when Mom was released. Mom had not eaten much since Monday and remained on a liquid diet. Her swallowing and other voluntary responses were diminishing as her organs began to work less effectively.

After the doctor completed her rounds, she came back to Mom's room.

"Do you want to take care of your mother at home?" she asked.

Of course, my response was "Yes." Mom wanted to be in a familiar space with her family when it was her time to leave.

This option was both unexpected and welcome. I was sure Mom's angels intervened and facilitated this option for us.

I was eager to take Mom home, but the move would have to wait until after the weekend as it was early afternoon on Friday and all the arrangements could not be completed in the remaining workday. Home Care had to make arrangements for delivery of a hospital bed and oxygen and assign a support nurse for Mom's care.

I was so excited when I told Mom that she could come to my house to stay with me as long as she wanted once arrangements were made. She smiled a weak smile and grasped my hand tightly saying she could hardly wait.

I immediately called my family and told them that Mom could come to the acreage and we could look after her there. My sisters were as thrilled as I was. They were in transit by car as airplane travel was not sanctioned due to COVID-19. One was travelling from British Columbia and the other from Ontario. I was relieved they would be here soon. Unfortunately my brother was unable to come, which he found devastating.

Over the past few days, I had spent as much time as I was allowed with Mom and talked with the doctors and hospital staff about Mom's condition and care. Like Mom, I had not slept well and was mentally drained. After the doctor asked if I wanted to take Mom home, the gravity of the situation began to sink in.

Mom did not want intrusive end-of-life intervention, only comfort measures. My family and I had discussed her decision with the doctors in the early hours of Tuesday morning when we were considering the pacemaker implant. I reminded myself that at that time, the doctor told us our Mother could live a few days, a few weeks, or a few months. I hadn't considered until now that the shortest time was most likely. I was suddenly struck with panic, fear, and anguish at the thought of Mom actually dying ... and very soon. But not before she came to the acreage as she wished.... I hoped and prayed.

Between the IV and antibiotics, Mom had bursts of energy throughout the day and evening and the calls with family continued. Her music played softly in the background, and she sang a word or two or hummed as she could. The music soothed her.

I was allowed to again sleep overnight in her room and we joked about the fact that I was once more sleeping in the chair while she got the comfortable bed. She still had a sense of humour but reminded me she wanted to sleep over at the acreage. I could finally say that she could come and sleep over at the acreage, but not until three more nights at the hospital. She sighed and gave me a weak smile, gently squeezed my hand and said a quiet, "Thank you. I want to stay at your house."

During the night, Mom's sleep was interrupted by cries of pain; the nurses gave her pain medication, after which she rested more easily. Several times, she called out to check if I was still there. I would go to her bedside, stroke her face, kiss her cheeks, and hold her hand while she tried to go back to sleep. During stress-free periods, she would hum along to some of the music as it played softly.

This night, while I watched Mom struggle with life, I remembered how active Mom had been in the lives of her children and grandchildren. Though Mom was a working mother, she made efforts to attend significant life and school events and sports activities for all of us. She spent countless hours at school functions and extracurricular activities, watching her children and grandchildren. Once she retired, she participated even more. She was the story reader, cookie baker, and cheerleader for us and our children. When she visited our homes for a few weeks, she was the gardener, baker, cabbage roll maker, and Swiffer™ lady. We all loved to have her.

I was comforted knowing Mom had faith and prayer in her life and I admired her quiet and humble confidence. She would think about matters that troubled her, and if she could not find a resolution, after some time, she would say, "I have to let that go," meaning that the Lord would eventually suggest a solution. She was a woman of prayer and patience; ultimately, she received what she asked for or needed. Recalling Mom's life in this context lifted my downheartedness. I had always thought I was so fortunate to have such a mother, a woman who embraced motherhood and unconditional love. I was so sad that she would be gone soon, but so happy I had her in my life as my mom for so long.

Saturday

I left the hospital mid-morning and returned in the early afternoon. Wanda had arrived late the previous night from Ontario and Winnifred would be arriving from British Columbia that afternoon. They needed to have special permission and complete COVID-19 testing before visiting Mom, and they set about getting tested and approved.

I had not been back at the hospital very long when, to my surprise, I turned to find Wanda at the door of Mom's room. I was so excited that she was there and could see Mom. I quickly helped her sanitize, put on the required gown and mask, and she rushed in to see Mom. There were tears of joy and relief as Mom and Wanda embraced. It was a gentle yet intensely emotional reconnection of mother and daughter. An urgent yet soft meeting of hearts. After a few minutes of embrace, my sister talked with Mom, soothing her, and the joy in Mom's heart was evident by the slight smile on her face.

Unfortunately, it was only a short time before a nurse came along and questioned my sister regarding her presence in the hospital during pandemic restrictions. My sister had followed the rules, but unfortunately the documentation of her approval to enter the hospital had not yet been forwarded by the proper authorities and she was required to leave the hospital until her status was confirmed. Nonetheless, she was thrilled and satisfied to have spent even those few minutes with Mom.

Mom was alert and attentive some of the day. She had been more alert the past two days and carried on conversations with family and nursing staff. However, even this minimal interaction required her to expend considerable energy, and her body and mind were weary. She was still not eating and was only taking jellied water. Fluids, antibiotics, and pain meds were administered as necessary through IV.

In the late afternoon, Winnifred was finally approved to visit and came to see Mom. It was another reunion of mother and daughter, as tears of joy and relief flowed again. Mom's spirit was re-energized as she hugged and talked with Winnifred. Her heart was overflowing with love.

When my sisters were now officially approved to visit, they made a schedule to sit with Mom. I had been able to spend time at the hospital with Mom while my sisters were in transit, and now they took turns at the hospital, with me relieving them when needed.

They took over the night vigil, sleeping in the

recliner chair beside Mom's bed. One night, while Wanda was at the hospital, she was concerned about Mom's laboured breathing. Worried that Mom would not make it through the night, she called Winnifred to the hospital. This traumatic episode alarmed my sisters, who then both spent most of the night with Mom until her breathing normalized. They were so relieved Mom would live to see another day.

Sunday

After my sisters' arrived, Mom had a renewed spark; she was more aware and alert. Her spirit was elevated and she was excited that in one more sleep, she would be moved to the acreage.

I sat with her for a few hours while my sisters organized themselves for their stays with Mom at the hospital for the next 24 hours and then later at the acreage. Mom was still on oxygen and pain meds intravenously. She was aware of her surroundings when awake but slept most of the morning and afternoon. When awake, we chatted, but she found lengthy conversations used up all her energy, so she preferred to say only a few words and listen to others talk to her. She was looking forward to being at the acreage where all her daughters would be with her.

My sisters comforted and cared for Mom in the evening and during the night. They applied lotion to her dry skin and gently rubbed her feet and hands, and she relaxed to their touch. They talked, laughed, cried, and prayed with her. They sang and played music they knew she liked, noticing that sometimes she tried to tap her toes like she often would do when the music moved her. They heard her humming along to some of the music. They were elated when they had even a short conversation with her, cherishing each time Mom told them, "I love you too."

Monday

The morning was hope-filled with the anticipation of Mom's move to the acreage. Each of us sisters had tasks to ensure the transfer went smoothly. I was at the hospital before 8 a.m. Winnifred, who had been at the hospital for the last part of the night, went to the acreage to rest. Wanda came to the hospital to stay with Mom while I worked on confirming Mom's transfer preparations. I was waiting for confirmation from the social worker that arrangements would be made this day for transportation by ambulance to the acreage and that Home Care was prepared to provide the necessary orientation and ongoing support for Mom's care after the move. I needed to phone and physically track down the individuals needed to facilitate the move. The transfer needed to happen as quickly as possible so Mom could be in familiar and comfortable surroundings with her family.

I slipped in and out of Mom's room to brief Wanda. Mom was sleeping off and on and was becoming anxious about the delay. Finally, in the late afternoon, it was confirmed. Everything was in place. The staff pulled out all the stops to make the move happen as planned. Our family was relieved and grateful.

Home to the Acreage

Mary's "Retreat"
Wanita's acreage near Holbein, Saskatchewan

On Monday, May 3, 2021, Home Day, Wanda and I stayed at the hospital with Mom while Winnifred remained at the acreage and coordinated Home Care delivery of the hospital bed and other supplies required for our mom's care.

There was some confusion and delay in transferring Mom from the bed in her hospital room into the ambulance transport bed. She was fretful and Wanda and I tried to assure her that she would be taken by ambulance and we would meet her at the acreage. Initially, we thought one of us could ride in the ambulance with Mom to keep her calm, but we were told that could not happen.

Wanda and I were to meet the ambulance in the hospital parking lot and they would follow us to the acreage. So off we went, our bewildered and frazzled Mom and the ambulance attendants following behind. Somehow I lost the ambulance that was supposed to follow us but the driver found his way to the acreage without our guidance.

Generally, at this time of year, when Mom and I travelled to the acreage, she scanned the ditches for crocuses. I shared her joy of spotting the first one of the season; it meant spring was finally here. This drive was unlike any Mom or I had experienced, and there would be no joyful sightings of crocuses.

As we travelled, Wanda and I discussed how

COURAGE AND A CASTLE

Mom wanted to come to the acreage to live with me at the beginning of COVID-19 and why that hadn't worked out. At the time, when we considered the option, there had been thorough discussions with the care home owner, health officials, Mom's doctor and family members about what would happen if she got COVID-19 or my husband and/or I got COVID-19 while Mom was in our care. We would not be able to return Mom to her care home during the pandemic if we took her to the acreage and could not care for her. As a family, after weighing all the options, we had decided it was best for her to remain in the care home during COVID-19, even though visitation was limited. (As it turned out, I fell and broke my hip a few days into January 2021 and required immediate surgery. By the time Mom fell in late April 2021, I was fully mobile but not entirely back to regular activity.)

My sister and I agreed that we made the right decision for Mom's care back then, and now it was the right decision for Mom to get her wish and come to the acreage where her three daughters could care for her as long as she lived. We felt blessed to have this opportunity.

Wanda and I arrived at the acreage a few minutes before the 6:30 p.m. arrival of the ambulance. As we could not ride in the ambulance with Mom to temper her journey, on arrival, she was disoriented and distressed, with only the dishevelled hospital gown covering her. Her hair was wild, which matched the look of fear in her eyes that darted furtively, searching for a familiar face. She flailed her hands and squirmed in the gurney as the attendants lifted her out of the ambulance, up the back step, and into the back door landing. She made urgent-sounding throaty noises to voice her panic. As the ambulance attendants moved the gurney through the doorway into the living room, Winnifred gently squeezed Mom's hand and stroked her forehead, and said, "Mom, you are at the acreage now. Wanita and Wanda and I will stay with you. You can have as many sleepovers as you like. We will look after you. Isn't that great, Mom? We all get to be at the acreage together." Then she gently kissed Mom on the forehead.

Once Mom saw my sister's familiar face, heard her soothing words, and felt her touch, her panic faded, and she began to relax. Mom was at the acreage where she wanted to be, a place that brought her comfort. After each of us reassured Mom that she was at the acreage, we were all there with her and we would look after her, Mom, now less distressed, settled in her hospital bed in the middle of the living room, warm blankets tucked around her.

Over the fall and winter, before my hip mishap, my husband and I had refreshed the main floor of our house, including Mom's room, which doubled as my office. I had painted her room a soft grey and made curtains to match her new bedspread, which was white with baby blue trim and abstract blue and pink flowers splashed on green stems. I had shown Mom pictures of her newly painted and decorated room, but she had not been able to sleep over in her updated bedroom because of the onset of the pandemic. And now she could not sleep in her refreshed room because the hospital bed could not fit through her bedroom door. Instead, she was in a hospital bed in the living room, with its vaulted ceiling and wall-to-wall windows facing the forest and greening yard. She liked the acreage in springtime.

It was as if we had just painted the walls soft grey and redecorated the living room for Mom's presence. The new off-white and grey drapes and white sheers let in the warm sunlight in a spa-like setting. Mom had often remarked that she liked coming to the acreage as it felt like being at a relaxing retreat. It was no wonder that she wanted to be there; it was peaceful, and all her daughters could have sleepovers with her for as long as she wanted. She would spend the last few days of her life feeling at home.

Mom settled in the hospital bed, still uncomfortable. My sisters, their husbands, my husband and I took turns welcoming Mom to the acreage and sharing words of love and comfort with her. My husband had returned home from work shortly before Mom arrived in the ambulance. My sisters' husbands came to the acreage to greet Mom. Later that evening, Wanda's husband went to Prince Albert and Winnifred's husband went on to Saskatoon, allowing my sisters to focus on taking care of our mother in her last days. None of us had tested positive for COVID-19, and we were hopeful that our limited contact with others would allow us to interact safely with Mom and each other.

Mom was in considerable pain and agitated from the ambulance ride, though she was relieved to be at the acreage. Thankfully, the Home Care nurse arrived soon after the ambulance attendants left and brought the oxygen equipment Mom required for ease of breathing. Mom was much more comfortable not having to gasp for air. Next, the nurse attached the line that delivered the pain medication to Mom intravenously and gave her pain medication. This relaxed Mom enough for the nurse to rearrange the sheets on the bed and then remove Mom's catheter. There was no longer a need for it as Mom was no longer taking in liquids or food, not even jellied water; she was only accepting a wet swabbing of her mouth.

The Home Care nurse talked directly to Mom, including her in the conversation, and explained what she was doing as she worked. She spoke with us as she gently, and with the greatest of care, attended to Mom. As the nurse worked, Mom's tension began to diminish; it was clear Mom knew where she was, who was there, and that she would spend the rest of her days at the acreage.

As she tended to Mom, the Home Care nurse taught us what we were required to do to provide support and comfort. We learned to press the button to deliver the pain medication if Mom cried out or looked uncomfortable. There was no limit to the frequency of pressing the button. We learned it was metered and could not deliver too much medication, no matter how many times we pushed it. So if Mom looked uncomfortable, we understood it was just fine to press the button. We were all very pleased; we did not want Mom in pain.

We learned to check and ensure her oxygen was appropriately connected to ease her breathing and to rub the special cream on her nose to better tolerate the hard plastic device. We did not have to turn the gauge; it was set at the appropriate level, and the Home Care nurse would check it each time she came. We were taught how to sponge bathe Mom just as the hospital nurses had, doing one part of the body at a time, drying it and covering it so that she would not become chilled. We learned to continuously moisten her mouth with swabs to keep her mouth slightly damp, for comfort. No food or water was required. Her body was past the point of accepting anything into it. Her organs were shutting down slowly.

My sisters understood the process of changing the bed sheets, frequently turning Mom and propping her with pillows to provide support, more than I did, so they coached me when I assisted with those tasks. Mom was always cold, so flannelette sheets and cozy fuzzy blankets warmed her, as did the sunshine that shone through the large living room windows on her now frail body. Comfort measures and ease of passage measures were all we could offer Mom now. She was letting go peacefully; we knew she was letting go, and each of us told her in our own way that it was okay for her to leave whenever she was ready... but none of us was really prepared to have our mother go. We tried attentively and earnestly to comfort Mom and reciprocate the care and unconditional love she had shown us in her lifetime.

After the Home Care nurse left and Mom was comfortable, we realized that none of us had eaten; we were wrapped up learning what we needed to know to look after Mom. As all our husbands were still at the acreage, we had a late evening, impromptu barbeque with a toast to Mom being at the acreage.

Then, we organized who was sleeping and sitting up with Mom overnight and discussed what other things needed to be done over the next few days. We did not ask our husbands to sit with Mom, though they were welcome to visit her.

My sisters and I were relieved to finally have Mom with us at the acreage. We were thankful to have her with us and to be able to comfort and care for her during these last few days of her well-lived, earthly life. Now, even with COVID-19 still rampant, she was with family again, at the acreage where she wanted to be.

Although caring for our beloved mother was a privilege and an honour, it was not without challenges. Some challenges were met better than others, but we remained united in our love of Mom and our collective desire to support her with a safe and loving environment where she could peacefully prepare herself for her journey to the "world without end" that her abiding faith inspired.

As my sisters had been at the hospital the previous evening with little sleep, we agreed that I would start the night with Mom, and each of them would take a later turn during the night.

During my time with Mom, I puttered with quiet household tasks and sat and had tea at Mom's bedside with the moon shining through the window. I said, "Thank you for being my Mother." I told her I loved her and appreciated all the care and love she provided me and my family. I told her I didn't want her to go but that when it was her time, she should not be bound by my sadness about her leaving, as I would love her forever.

I tucked her blanket around her, hugged and kissed her cheek and forehead, and stroked her grey, frazzled hair. I played her music softly, including the songs and melodies she loved and used to tap her toes to. I was happy Mom was in a place she found comforting and home-like with my sisters and me to love and care for her in her final days.

As Mom slept, I made two lists — one for me and one for one of my sisters — of phone calls and other tasks that needed to be done the following day. I left the two lists on the table clearly marked along with the necessary papers for the calls.

The following day, I awoke to find Wanda, who had no list, saying she had nothing to do, so she would go and clean Mom's room at the care home. This set me off, ranting that our sole purpose in having Mom with us was to spend time with her and care for her while she was still alive and that her room could be cleaned out after she was no longer here. A heated and emotional exchange occurred, which resulted in hurt feelings between me and my sister. Once the conflict eased, I thought about how people deal with death and stressful situations differently. I failed to realize that Wanda's way of dealing with difficult situations is to clean and keep physically busy. That was Mom's way as well.

In the end, Mom's room was not cleared out that day and Wanda spent the day with Mom, Winnifred, and me. I was upset that Mom, who was trying to leave us peacefully, had to be subjected to our quarrelling at this sensitive time of her passage, but I found comfort in knowing that Mom was always good at blocking out the "noise" of life and staying on track with the task; I hoped that she had done so this day.

Any remaining tension of Tuesday's start to the day remained in check and we three sisters spent the day providing comfort and care to our mother. When the Home Care nurse called mid-morning, we had already given Mom a sponge bath and changed her sheets. We had moved her routinely to avoid bed sores and so that she would be more comfortable. We had pressed the button for pain medication to be delivered when we saw her in discomfort. When we gathered at the dining room table for coffee or snacks, we pulled Mom, in her hospital bed, near. When we sat in the living room, we rearranged the location of the chairs and her bed so we could be close to each other and include Mom in the conversation.

We sisters sat together with Mom in view and

reminisced, through laughter and tears, about our lives with her. In the last year of Mom's life, because of COVID-19 restrictions, we arranged for the care home staff to facilitate video calls with Mom from her tablet. During those video calls, Mom would randomly press the buttons, and suddenly, everyone would be wearing a hat, a strange-looking mustache, or a misshaped head. Once, Mom turned herself into a kitten that would "Meow" repeatedly and speak in a kitty voice. We could not stop laughing, and neither could Mom. She had no idea what she had done or how to undo it, so the rest of the video had Mom looking and sounding like a kitty.

We were connected to Mom, who was open and intuitive. For most of our lives, we would often get a phone call from her to check how we were, as somehow she knew we had a difficult matter to deal with. She did not press for information but offered guidance, support, wisdom, and unconditional love. She was an ever-welcome presence of strength in the lives of her family. Her usual greeting was a hug upon arrival, a hug and kiss when you left, and an affectionate "Love You, Miss You, God Bless You."

We lamented that for the last few years of Mom's life, when Alzheimer's overtook her, we no longer had that same connection. Fortunately for us, she did remember her children, but she did not recall our daily contact. She would often not recall phone calls or visits. I would get loudly-spoken, curt phone messages, "Hi, it's Mother. I haven't seen you for a long time. Call me right away. Love you." When in reality, I had just left.

In the past few years, when asked how her day was, she would reply, "So far, so good," with a smile. She would also say, "Thank you for being my daughter," or "my son," or "my son-in-law," or "granddaughter," whatever the case, with a "love you" to follow. She had other phrases she routinely mentioned like "My mother-in-law did not like yellow flowers, but I do." You never knew what memory she would randomly recall and how she would relate to it.

We marvelled at Mom's perpetual faith and consistent prayer. Though her life was filled with obstacles and struggles, she believed the Lord was her Shepherd. Psalm 23:1-6 — *The Lord is my Shepherd* — was one of her favourite prayers. Mom had told us many times that her faith and prayer helped her find peace and strength to live as best she could without her mother, her husband, and her sons. Her resilience, vigour, and courage were traits we valued; despite life's tragedies, her heart and mind were always open to accepting new challenges gracefully. We admired her ability to embrace life, adapt to change, and welcome each new day with gratitude, even with Alzheimer's.

We were comforted remembering how she

supported us physically and emotionally as we moved out of (and sometime back into) the family home, sought higher education, took on different careers, struggled after relationships fell apart, lost employment, or moved to another city. Mom said we were all individuals and needed different things. She knew and understood us and welcomed whatever the new iteration of our individual families were.

We talked to each other and to Mom. She interacted very little, but her hearing, as usual, was extraordinary, and we felt she was processing what she heard. Sometimes, she would say a few words and try to smile, but mostly, she kept her eyes closed and would acknowledge she heard you by a slight movement or a soft sound. She managed to say, "I love you too" several times during conversations. We laughed and cried at some of our recollected stories. We played her favourite music in the background, trying to set a cheerful yet peaceful atmosphere for her. To our delight, every so often, Mom would hum a few bars or manage to sing a few words.

My sisters devotedly rubbed her feet, back, hands and head while softly talking to her. This soothed Mom. They could feel the tension drain from her body when they massaged her. We prayed with and for her and connected via video with our brother Wayne, who was willing but unable to make the trip during the pandemic. As Wayne prayed Mom's favourite prayers, occasionally Mom seemed to try to mouth the words.

After praying, he said, "Thank you for being my mother. I love you."

Mom was able to muster a whispered, "I love you too." We all cried.

One of my sons called on video, talked with Little Gram, and told her he loved her. Though she was primarily wordless that day, she coaxed her mouth to a protruding "O" as if to blow a kiss to him, and we all cried again with joy.

Mid-afternoon, the Home Care nurse came to see how Mom was doing and found her resting peacefully in her hospital bed in the living room, with sunshine warming her as she nestled under her cozy blankets. She said she was heartened and delighted with how we cared for Mom. She told us that upon entering the house, she felt peaceful and could see that Mom was at ease and surrounded by love.

She checked Mom's vital signs, oxygen, and pain medication and looked at her skin for any sore spots. My sisters were complimented for the moisturizing massages. She spent time talking to us and Mom about Mom's life and how our mother came to be at the acreage with us caring for her. The nurse told us Mom was very fortunate to have daughters who would look after her in her last days with so much love. We told her we felt blessed that, despite the pandemic, we could come together and have Mom with us for the last days of her life.

During the day, we made the necessary calls to initiate the plans for the after-life processes, which involved navigating the restrictions for Celebrations of Life due to COVID-19. We discussed and began making decisions regarding the service, music, readings, flowers, obituary, and burial. None of those conversations were easy, but all were necessary to prepare a fitting send-off for our beloved mother.

On a lighter side, at tea time in the afternoon, we recalled playing Bingo with Mom by video during the pandemic. All family members were sent bingo cards, and whoever tuned in would play along. The care home staff would tune Mom in on her tablet. One brother-in-law was usually the caller. Before he called three numbers, Mom would shout out, "BINGO!"

We would say, "No, Ma, you can't have a Bingo already."

"Oh," she would say.

He would call a few more numbers and Mom would call "BINGO!" After reviewing the numbers called, most of the time, she was correct. She had a Bingo.

The winners were given a Loonie when they played Bingo at the care home. Mom would say she should get a Loonie for winning on video Bingo. So, I would drop off her winnings in an envelope when I was allowed to visit through the door. Mom had a little pink wallet full of Loonie Bingo winnings. So naturally, she took pleasure in adding her video Bingo winnings to her already bulging pink wallet. This story made us laugh, Mom sure loved Bingo and cards.

At supper, we again pulled Mom and her hospital bed to the dining room table and had a toast to her day with us. We took turns sitting up with Mom during the night. I sat with Mom first and planned, preparing three new lists for the next day, one for each of us sisters, and left them on the table clearly marked with our names.

I spoke to Mom again about her leaving and said I wouldn't like it when she was ready to let go, but I could accept it. From my sisters, I learned that they also shared private moments with Mom and told her the same thing. We were not ready to let her go, but we would learn to accept it.

As had been the case for all the nights I spent with Mom, this night, I played music. The playlist I had made began with an instrumental tune I didn't recall selecting. As it played, I thought it might be too "busy" for her as she seemed to be quietly readying herself for passing peacefully, and I didn't want to interrupt her journey. As I watched her reaction, she remained calm and peaceful, so I let it play.

A few days later, it wore on me that I let it play, so I looked up the meaning of the German title, "*Augenblicke der Liebe*," and found the title translates to *Moments of Love* in English. I thought that Mom's angel must have put it on the playlist and let me play it to ease her passage; it was a fitting song to signify how much we loved her and that her love was everlasting and unconditional. I was comforted and understood that Mom was recalling all the "moments of love" from her life as the music played.

At about 3:30 a.m., Wanda came to sit with Mom. I kissed Mom and my sister goodnight and went to a fretful sleep.

Heaven

Mary

One is never ready, even when it is time ...

Suddenly, at 7:15 a.m. on May 5, 2021, my husband woke me and told me to come with him; he thought my mom had died. In an instant, I was out of bed and running to the living room. Beside Mom's bed, my two sisters and my husband stood, staring at Mom in disbelief. She was gone from our world.

Leaving for work, my husband had passed through the living room to say goodbye to Mom. He stopped at her bedside and said, "Good morning, Mary. I am going to work now. See you at lunch."

He did not expect a response, but his mother-in-law's stillness pushed him to say to my sisters, "I don't think Mary is breathing."

My sisters had just stepped away from attending Mom and were in the kitchen getting coffee, still in full view of her, as our mother took her last breath and quietly and peacefully slipped away.

Winnifred was disturbed and troubled by his statement. "She can't be gone so quickly and quietly," she said anxiously. "We were just there saying good morning."

"She was softly breathing a moment ago. I just finished rubbing her feet and hands, and she was breathing fine," Wanda offered with grave concern.

The two sisters looked at one another, bewildered.

COURAGE AND A CASTLE

They rushed to Mom's bedside, and put their hands on her chest and felt no heartbeat. Alarmed, they put their fingers under her nose and by her mouth feeling for breath and there was none. My sisters stood in shock, and my husband hurried to wake me and tell me that my mother had just died.

Many years ago, I heard that once a person stops breathing, they can still hear for two minutes. So, on this day, at this time, as we wept softly, we all found solace in that notion and huddled around Mom to kiss and hug her and stroke her hands, face, and hair. Out loud, we told her that we loved her dearly and that it was okay for her to go. We thanked her for being our mother.

For the next several hours, we went through the motions, doing what needed to be done but not really believing that our dear mother was gone from us forever. Although we knew it was true that she had died, at that moment, we could not grasp that she would never hug us again, share her words of wisdom, or make us smile with her humour. Oh no, it could not be true.

We called the Home Care nurse. While she was en route, my sisters and I made heartbreaking calls to family. In between my sisters and I making calls, my son, who video-called the night before with Little Gram, called to see how things were this morning. With Mom lying lifeless in front of us, we were about to toast her passing to "the world without end," as our mother certainly was in Heaven. He was invited to join our send-off of Little Gram. Now, together with my sisters and me, he acknowledged and shared in our toast to celebrate our new Heavenly Mother.

"Love You, Miss You, God Bless You," we said as we pictured our beautiful mother smiling at us from her rightful Heavenly home. We hailed in unison, *"Thank You For Being Our Mother* and Little Gram." Then we held up our little shot glasses of brandy, clinked them together, and drank to the peaceful passing of our mom. Winnifred rubbed brandy on Mom's lips to include her in our celebration. Even though it was before noon, Mom would have enjoyed the spontaneity and the toast with Hungarian brandy.

The Home Care nurse arrived shortly after our celebration and readied Mom's now quiet body for the funeral home staff to come and take her for cremation. As we spoke with the nurse, she completed her tasks with care. We shared our experience of the impact of the pandemic on our mom and how it had aged her. As her daughters, we expressed our gratitude that we could care for Mom at the acreage she considered her retreat home for her final days. We thanked the Home Care nurse for the support she offered Mom and us through the past few days. In turn, she told us that though it was sad that our mom passed, it was heartwarming, seeing the attentiveness and love we surrounded her with during her last few days. We all agreed we were blessed to be a part of Mom's life.

The Home Care nurse had just left when the staff from the funeral home arrived to carry Mom's body away. They, too, were very respectful of Mom. We hugged and kissed her one last time before they wrapped her in a silken cloth and took her away. Winnifred said she could still taste the brandy she had lovingly rubbed on Mom's lips as she kissed her last goodbye. The funeral home staff left a sympathy card and a red rose, which was fitting, considering Mom's affinity for red roses.

Though we were emotionally spent and running on adrenaline, we had the laundry done and put away, and the living room furniture back in place before lunch — as if Mom had not even been there. It was surreal.

Life and death during the pandemic were disheartening and melancholy. Arranging a Celebration of Life service for Mother presented many challenges one would not have had to consider in non-COVID times and created additional distress. As we were all grieving the loss of our beloved mother, as we planned her service, tensions rose and fell with our raw emotions.

We decided where and when the Celebration of Life would be held. Who could attend was a difficult decision as, at that time, only twelve people were allowed at a funeral; thankfully, the funeral home offered a live streaming.

The answer to the question of what kind of vessel should lovingly hold Mom's ashes came to us as we sat at the kitchen table and looked around; the pickle crock on top of the cupboard that she used for homemade pickles spoke to us. Over the years, Mom had used this earthenware container for pickling vegetables at the acreage. She said the crock brought back fond memories of how she and her mother would pickle vegetables in a big wooden barrel. So, placing her remains in an object she had an emotional attachment to seemed fitting.

More and more questions arose for discussion and decision. What about her obituary? How could we fully represent her remarkable life in a few short words? Who would officiate? What special prayers would she like to be said, and by whom? What were her favourite songs, and which versions did we want to be included? Who would like to speak about Mom?

Some plans were agreed upon quickly, while

others took longer and created tension. There were so many details to try and get right to celebrate the life of our mom, whom we all loved so dearly. When frustration overtook us, we reminded ourselves how fortunate we were to be able to have Mom in our care for the last few days of her life. That brought us comfort.

Mom's earthly body was cremated, and we three sisters collected her ashes on Friday, May 7th, 2021. Each of Mom's children respectfully accepted some of her ashes and the remainder were placed in the antique two-tone brown, earthenware pickle crock.

Mom was returned to the acreage in the brown crock and placed on the dining room table where she would be included in our daily activities and conversations.

Mother's Day was Sunday, May 9, and we sisters and our husbands arranged to celebrate and honour Mom with a meal — our last Mother's Day with Mom. However, there was a misunderstanding before dinner, which brought on a dynamic exchange.

Grief and stress manifest in unexpected ways. A moratorium was undertaken, and harmony replaced hostility as we three sisters and our husbands sat together with Mom's ashes in the pickle crock adorning the dining room table. We toasted to Mom's new journey and agreed that Mom was now dancing with Dad to their favourite song, "Somewhere My Love." Finding balance and acceptance was fittingly attributed as the work of our mother.

We decided to finalize arrangements for Mom's service over the phone and after our Mother's Day celebration, my sisters and their husbands left, one to the lake and then to Saskatoon, the other directly to Saskatoon. We all needed some personal space to process our grief. Wayne continued his support via telephone. We were all emotionally drained and heartbroken.

My husband and I took the antique pickle crock with Mom's ashes to the chapel on Tuesday, May 11, 2021, the day of her Celebration of Life. We often drove the highway to Saskatoon with Mom as our passenger, but never like this day. Usually, there was coffee and Timbits with polka music playing and Mom humming or singing along while she tapped her toes. Maybe she was sipping her coffee, eating Timbits, tapping her toes and singing to the music, but from Heaven.

As we neared the chapel, my tears started flowing, and a wave of sorrow shrank my body. I carried the pickle crock with Mom's ashes into the vestibule and left her with the funeral director.

My sisters and I surveyed the memorial at the front of the chapel. A beautiful picture of Mom graced the stand covered with one of her favourite red scarves. A portrait of the Bessborough Hotel, where she worked to support her family, stood prominently beside it. Other items of meaning to her rested on the scarf: a well-worn prayer book and a rosary, her little pink wallet containing bingo winnings, glasses, a puzzle book, cards, and dice. Red roses peeked over her picture as if they knew they would bring her joy.

Some of her favourite songs, including "You Are My Sunshine" and "Somewhere My Love," played as we gathered. As we began down the aisle, "Make Me A Channel of Your Peace" filled the small chapel. Wanda reverently carried the ashes of Mom in the earthenware crock and placed it on the stand near the altar. We all took our seats for the Celebration of Mom's Life.

A Father from the church our family first attended in Saskatoon performed the service. He spoke of Mom as a woman of faith, unconditional love, and a servant of the Lord, an example of a humble, yet courageous and devoted, woman. His words brought comfort.

Via video, Wayne genuinely and heartfully expressed thankfulness for having our wonderful and loving mother. With reverent sentiment, he read Mom's favourite prayer, Psalm 23, "The Lord is My Shepherd." Our hearts were aching from loss, but we were soothed when he avowed, "Thank you for being our mother."

Memorial for Mary
Wanita's acreage
May 2021

During the service, "Ava Maria" and "Mary In The Morning" filled the air, the melodies bringing tears and memories of moments of love. As the service ended, the polka, "Wooden Heart" played as Winnifred carried Mom's urn. As my sister began her exit, she danced a few polka steps in reverence to Mom, and my other sister, Wanda, took up the steps, polka-dancing our mother out of the room. Mom would have been happy with the choice of music and would have said "Amen" to dancing her out of the chapel.

As the gravesite was outdoors, more family and friends were welcome to pay their respects to Mom. The life she lived was celebrated as she was laid to rest with her husband and son. Each daughter placed a keepsake into the box containing the antique pickle crock that embraced Mom's ashes, as did grandchildren and great-grandchildren. Red roses were placed on her grave site to symbolize love and because they were her favourite flowers.

For my siblings and me, there was no doubt that Mom went to Heaven. She embodied a life of servitude and, through her faith, showed us the virtues of selflessness, forgiveness, kindness, love, and acceptance. Motherhood was a life-long journey that she championed through her boundless, unconditional love for us — her children — just as she loved her husband without question.

For Mom, faith and hard work were foundations enfolded in her daily life. She always received what she needed through hard work and prayer and greeted each day with gratitude. Her life was filled with challenges, and her strength and resilience deepened as she overcame them. Embracing faith created acceptance, an openness to change, and the ability for her to learn and adapt. She never stopped learning, loving, and being grateful. The way she lived her life and the joy and humour of her character made her a role model and inspiration for us and others.

With the name "Mary," combined with her strong faith, it was no wonder we lovingly teased her with the title "Holy Mary." Most certainly, Mom was welcomed to Heaven, no doubt her presence enhancing the spirits of all around her, just as her presence did on Earth. As a family, we are resolute that if ever there was a person deserving of a "Heavenly Afterlife," it was she. We picture her smiling at us from her eternal home.

Gifts From Mom

Wanita
in Mary's Bessborough sweatshirt
May 2021

Mom was very intuitive and listened to her surroundings. She believed that things were connected for a reason; you may not immediately know the reason you are prompted to do something, but sometimes later you would be given the opportunity to find out the rest of the story. This has been true many times since Mom's passing.

When we opened the cabin in late May 2021, I went through the bathroom, collecting Mom's personal care items. In her bedroom, I went through her closet, dresser, and night table, sorting through clothes, and other possessions she kept at the lake, setting aside some of them as keepsakes.

This was different from a usual lake summer. Due to COVID-19 restrictions, there were none of the typical family gatherings at the lake, but more notably, this would be the first summer without my ever-present mother, Mary, as she had passed away only weeks before at the age of ninety-seven.

Even though Mom had travelled to many places, she was always eager to spend weekends and holiday time at the lake with family members. For years, she had two daughters who had cabins at different lakes, and she had her choice of which lake to go to. Once Winnifred moved away, there was only one cabin to go to in the summer, our family cabin at Emerald Lake. At our cabin, Mom had her bedroom called "Little Gram's room." She was pampered at the lake, deservedly so. Sometimes, she would get breakfast served twice as she insisted she had yet to eat. She enjoyed the warmth of the sun and would sit on the deck, visit, and do her puzzles — or just watch whatever activity was happening on the lake. Sometimes, she would walk in the shallow water or sit on the bench by the beach.

Mary
Emerald Lake
2011

Even into her eighties, it was common for Mom to be on the paddle boat on the lake with one of her family. She went for boat rides until she was ninety-four; by that time, she found getting in and out of the boat too tricky. On cool evenings, you would see her sitting in front of the fireplace, watching the flames dance, and playing her puzzles on her tablet. After dark, she would play cards with family. This activity was accompanied by her old-time music and a drink of blueberry tea.

Mom was a good sport and contributed in any way she could; working with her was always pleasant, no matter the task. When she was younger, in her early eighties, she helped me stain the deck at the lake. The weather was hot and we had cold, wet facecloths under our sun hats. We drank iced tea, rested often, and finished the job together. Years later, we would still joke that it was not hot enough yet to stain the deck!

A few days after clearing Mom's bedroom, I went through a dresser upstairs and found a long-sleeved pullover sweatshirt, once bright white, now tainted yellow. I gently lifted it out of the drawer and shook it open. I pulled it to my face and inhaled deeply. There was no scent of my mother, but the sight and feel of the garment flooded my emotions with memories of her. It had the words *Bessborough Hotel* embossed on the front in black with an outline of the Bessborough Hotel above the lettering.

Mom had worked at the Bessborough Hotel and had taken enormous pride in her work at the "Castle on the River." She was a working mom before working moms were a thing. She retired as Head Housekeeper after thirty-one years of employment. Now, more than thirty years later, I discovered one of her mementos from her work life. I felt like Mom purposefully left it at the lake for me to find at this particular time.

Despite its faded state, it was in excellent repair. I slowly pulled it over me, and it felt like Mom was hugging me. Boy, did I ever need a hug from my mom! What a great find! What a great gift! I took it home, washed it in bleach, gave it a spritz of Mom's favourite White Diamond perfume and took a picture of myself in front of the fireplace at the lake wearing it. Later, I found pictures of Mom wearing her Bessborough sweatshirt. I treasure the sweatshirt — not only because it was Mom's but because of the significance of Mom's work at The Bessborough and how important that was for our family. Now, when I need a hug from Mom, I put on her Bessborough sweatshirt and feel her arms wrap around me like when I was a child.

December 2021 was not only my first Christmas without my mother being alive, with COVID-19, family gatherings were limited — a double whammy this Christmas. No Mother and no usual family gathering to share in Christmas.

My mother focused on the spiritual side of Christmas, and when she was alive, our family embraced it with her. Like my mother, I love Christmas time, when all the family gets together to bake and prepare food, decorate the house, set up the Christmas tree, and play Christmas music.

During those last eight years when Mom lived in the care home, she spent Christmas at the acreage with my family. She would help decorate the Christmas tree branches, but only up to a certain height due to her seated position. Her decorations were clustered at those lower levels; a fact commented on by one of my granddaughters. However, Mom was delighted she could still assist with decorating and it was always wonderful to have her.

While Mom and I decorated the tree, we listened to Christmas music and we often talked about Dad and his Christmas tree light ritual. He would stretch out the strings of lights across the floor, plug them in, check each bulb, replace those needed, and then meticulously wrap them around the tree. I was Dad's helper with the Christmas tree lights and I learned to follow all his instructions carefully.

Besides a well-decorated lighted tree, Mom wished our house to be decorated for the holiday season, so red and green ribbons, bows, garland, and mistletoe were draped around the house. She wanted the paper Christmas card holder to display all the cards on the wall, so I placed the cardholder in full view of her usual chair. I baked her favourite shortbread cookies, and she dipped them in her tea after we finished our decorating. Christmas preparations were a fun-filled time together.

Each year, we took pictures of Mom dressed in a new festive Christmas outfit in front of the Christmas tree and made photo cards for her. Dressing her for the photos was easy as she always looked like a regal queen when she dressed up, with her natural silver-grey hair, red lipstick, and rouge. Unfortunately, once you pointed a camera at her, she strained her face, contorted her mouth, opened her eyes as if she was scared by a monster, and waited for you to press the button. She did not like her picture taken; she found it stressful to not close her eyes or hold her face in a certain position. It was quite the performance to behold. So, picture after picture had to be taken until she relaxed enough or she was caught her in a candid moment.

However, once a suitable picture was made into a Christmas postcard, Mom smiled joyfully. The magnificent "Smiling Mom" Christmas postcards would be inserted into the Christmas greeting cards she selected for each family member, having signed them with the corresponding "Love Mary," "Love Mother" or "Love Grandma". Though she took pleasure in sending the cards, as she aged, it was done over several days as she tired from selecting cards and signing her name repeatedly, all in one sitting.

Now, I only have sweet memories of Mom and Christmas preparations, and there is no one to delight in the story of my dad and his Christmas tree light routine. I was dreading my first Christmas without Mom.

During the years Mom lived in her personal care home, I usually visited her every other day. I became familiar with the residents Mom spent time with. They attended the dining room together for meals and tea and the activity room for daily events. Sometimes they would visit each other's rooms, and a few ladies liked to come to Mom's room to listen to her old-time music. Many of the other residents became familiar and friends with Mom. She developed a special bond with her card-playing ladies.

COURAGE AND A CASTLE

Mom did not understand everything concerning the pandemic or life in general. Alzheimer's was affecting her daily life and the isolation of the pandemic did not allow for daily contact with other people. A friend of my husband's, Frank, and his wife, Alice, lived in the same care home as Mom. Alice was still alert-minded. As I was not allowed to visit, and telephone conversations with Mom were difficult at best, I would call Alice, and she kept me current on the care home's activities and how Mom was doing. After those conversations, I would talk with Mom and then with staff if I needed them to check on a certain issue. It could be a simple thing such as her not knowing how to turn on the television or the location of her prayer book. It could be that she was feeling more tired and forgetful than usual and needed to be tested for a bladder infection. This method of information gathering worked well to facilitate care during the pandemic. Alice was pleased to help Mom and our family was grateful to have Alice to a go-between.

After Mom passed, I continued contact with Alice. She was coping with losing her lifelong partner, Frank, who passed away a few months before Mom. Though I communicated with Alice over the phone, I had not been at Mom's care home, where Alice also lived, since June.

Before Christmas of 2021, I was compelled

to go to the care home to feel reconnected with Mom. So, in mid-December, just before my first Christmas without Mom, I visited Alice, bringing along Tim Horton's coffee and Timbits for Alice and a tea for me — just as I would when I came to see Mom. I went by Mom's old room and said "Hi" through the closed door, knowing she was no longer living there. Then, I went to Alice's room; her walker was there, but she was not. I left the coffee, tea, and Timbits in her room and went to the dining room. The room was filled with residents sitting at tables and staff from all the floors. They were having a goodbye party for one of the staff, Zoey.

When I entered the room, the staff called my name and said, "Come in, join the party, and have lunch with us. We have a plate for you."

They gave me noodles, spring rolls, and cake. I told them I had no idea they were having a party, that I had just come to visit Alice. They said they saved me a chair right beside Alice. So, I took the plate offered, sat beside Alice, and enjoyed my lunch. I remarked to Alice that she never told me there was a party that afternoon as I would have picked a different day to visit. She said she did not know there was a party. At that point, I realized that Alice's memory had deteriorated significantly over the past few months. Also, she was now wheelchair-bound for events outside her room as her legs had lost strength.

I knew many residents who said they were happy to see me. Steve, the smiling man sitting on the other side of me, said he had not seen me for a long time. He said he missed my coming there. Other residents told me they still missed Mom and that she used to love playing cards, visiting, listening to music, and singing. I was touched emotionally being with the people Mom had lived with and the staff that had cared for her. Tears wavered at the edges of my eyelids, and a lump tightened my throat as we reminisced about Mom and talked about their lives. When I left, I went by Mom's old room again and thanked her for the lovely afternoon.

I had such an unexpected and heavenly afternoon. I am confident Mom had a hand in prompting me to go to the care home on that particular day. This party felt like the Christmas parties that I would share with Mom at the care home. It was heartwarming to feel so reconnected with the residents and the staff, and most especially connected to Mom. I had Christmas with Mom!

When I went to my car, I sat and wept uncontrollably. I was overwhelmed with a mixture of joy and sadness. I was so thankful to have had that beautiful experience just prior to my first Christmas without Mom. I thought of it as Mom's Christmas gift to me.

More recently, near the end of April 2023, at home on our acreage, I was prompted to leave my office and open the patio door, thinking I might have heard something. Upon opening the door, all was quiet. I closed the door and turned to go back to my office, but then stopped. I went back and opened the patio door again. I thought I heard kids yelling in the distance, but it couldn't be because it was a school day and it was just 11 a.m. I listened more carefully and heard a sound again; this time, I thought the sound was my husband Earl's voice. I put on my shoes and grabbed my phone. The dog and I headed toward the voice.

As I walked, my husband's voice became louder, yelling, "Come quick! I need you. I can't move! Hurry, Hurry, I need you!"

"I am coming as fast as I can. I'll be right there," I yelled, wondering what I would find when I arrived. Due to physical limitations, I cannot walk fast on uneven ground, but I hurried as fast as I could, without falling. Earl and I continued calling out to one another over the two minutes it took to get to his side.

When I arrived at the opening in the forest, the dog halted behind me. I saw my husband and quickly assessed the situation; he was trapped, the weight of the large farm tractor pushing the tractor's bucket edge against his legs and pinning him between the tractor bucket and the rear end of an old car. The edge of the tractor's bucket was cutting off the circulation in his left thigh. His right leg was also caught between the tractor bucket and the car's rear end, but was not being crushed, only pinned.

He quickly told me that he was trying to hook a chain from the tractor onto the old car when the tractor rolled forward and its bucket scooped up his legs and pinned him. He had no way to free himself and had left his cell phone in the shop. He said he started yelling for help, hoping someone would hear him and come and rescue him before he passed out from the pain. I was in the house, approximately a block away by city standards, when I felt the need to listen.

He was experiencing excruciating pain, still conscious, but colourless with fear. He asked me to free him by starting the tractor and rolling it backwards. I refused as I had no idea how to drive a tractor, and if the tractor lunged forward, his legs would be severed. After calling neighbours to come and assist me in freeing him, I found a metal stair rail in the immediate area and wedged it between the bucket and the car's rear end to reduce some of the pressure where the tractor bucket was putting the most force on his left thigh. This brought some immediate relief, and he said he could feel his circulation returning.

Two neighbours arrived and after a quick conversation about how to free my husband without further injury, we concluded that starting the tractor and having it lunge forward would sever his legs and therefore pulling the tractor backwards was the safest option. One neighbour, Garry, returned home to get his truck and a tow chain to pull the tractor backwards. This seemed to take forever, but my husband remained conscious and calm, though fearful and in severe pain. During the wait, our other neighbour, Rhonda, helped me continue to wedge the stair rail between the bucket and the car's rear to release pressure on my husband's pinned legs.

Garry returned and swiftly, yet carefully, hooked the chain to the tractor and pulled it backward. My husband jumped out of the bucket to safety on the ground. The dog ran to him as he laid there — trauma flowing out of his freed, but spent, body —

and began to apply happy dog kisses. My husband was freed and injured, but his leg was intact, and he could stand and walk.

All of us were relieved and grateful, none more so than my husband. I looked heavenward and said a heartfelt *thank you* to Mom, who had prompted me to go to the door and listen to my husband's call for help.

In Mom's life, her father nearly lost his arm when it was caught up in farm machinery while he worked alone in the field. After he managed to free himself from the equipment, he walked a mile to a neighbour's for help, holding his mutilated arm. Her father survived, and his arm was saved, though he had lifelong limitations from his injury. It was a traumatic event for the entire family. They were thankful he survived and would comment it was the stubborn German in him that made him walk to get help before finally collapsing.

Like her mother, my mother had a similar experience when her husband, my father John, had his arm caught in a mangle he was repairing when someone accidentally turned the motor on. That accident altered the course of my parents' lives and burdened my father with years of pain and countless surgeries, and cost him his dream of becoming a stationary engineer. However, Mom was ever grateful to still have her husband. She believed her prayers to spare her Johnny were answered in my dad's case, and that the Lord intervened.

In my case, with my husband on death's door, Mom intervened and triggered me to take action, stopping the cycle; the same fate did not befall my husband as it did her father and her husband. My husband had no lasting effects from his incident. Our neighbour removed him from harm's way. For that, my husband and I are grateful!

Though I continue to struggle with losing my mother, who has now been gone for more than four years. I know my siblings, her family, and her friends are also struggling. When I need a boost or an angel for protection, Mom intervenes in the most unusual ways, like prompting me to listen to my husband's voice or giving me a gift of a Christmas party. I find comfort in her interventions, protection, and messages of unconditional love.

She does the same for other family members.

As one of my sisters, Winnifred, was exercising alone in a new space, the songs playing were some of the old country songs our Mother used to hum along with. My sister was overtaken by the memories of Mom that the music evoked. She wept and hummed along as she exercised. She felt Mom's presence so strongly it was as if Mom was exercising and humming along with her! When she sees a butterfly, it reminds her of Mom and brings her comfort. Mom comes to my brother Wayne in prayer and continues to offer him guidance and strength. Pictures of Mom pop up on my sister Wanda's phone just when she needs a hug from Mom; she also feels Mom's presence when she is in her flower garden.

Our mom gave her children the gift of life, nurtured us, and guided us throughout our lives. She never stopped mothering, no matter her age, or our age. That is an incredible gift. So, it is common for us to have Mom still providing guidance, support, and unconditional love even though she is no longer on Earth.

Looking back, our mother set out many gifts for each of us to use throughout our lives. She shared and passed on teachings and attributes that were important to her: her hard work ethic, the importance of lifelong learning and education, her love of music, dance, playing cards, travel, and, most importantly, the significance of family and faith.

As children of Mary, regardless of our age, we had guidance and Mom's wisdom with us every day of her 74 years of mothering. That is a long time! And we are thankful to have enjoyed and experienced our time with our mother for so long. I am overjoyed that even now she continues to share her most precious gift with us—her everlasting, unconditional love!

Epilogue - May: The Month of Mary

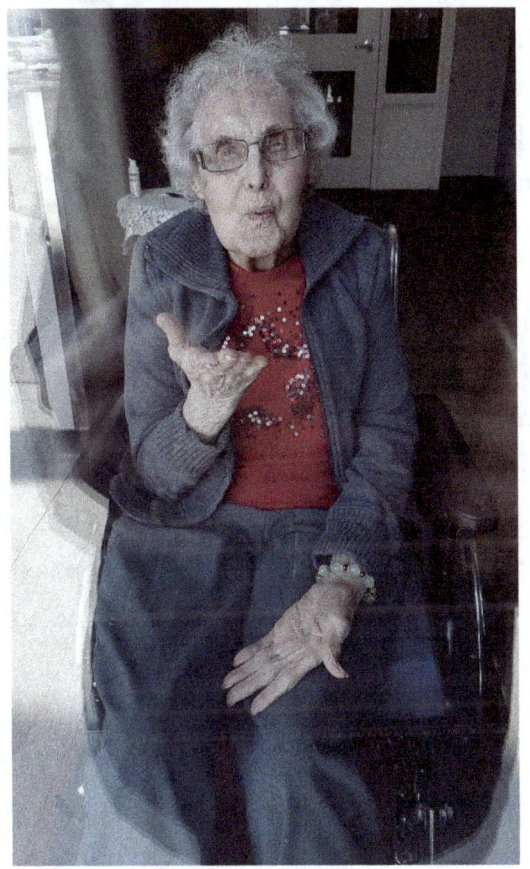

Mary
blowing a kiss
December 2020

Mom had a way of weaving things together. Her passing was no exception and things unfolded as they should.

May is the Month of Mary in the Catholic religion and the month of Mother's Day, when we celebrate the significance of our mothers in our lives. It was fitting that our mother would pass away in May — and she did so — on Wednesday, May 5, 2021.

Unsurprisingly, the qualities and virtues of the Virgin Mary and the attributes of motherhood are almost the same. My mother exemplified many of those characteristics. I am convinced that her passing in May is a testament to the woman she was — an intrinsically faithful, unconditionally loving, mother.

On May 19, 2022, our family had a mass to mark the first year of Mom's passing. Two of my cousins, Winnifred, Leslie (one of Mom's angels), a few members of the congregation, and I attended.

Looking back, it was as if Mom was weaving and connecting life events for us in her soft, subtle approach. She guided us through our sorrow to a happier day, knowing that her time with us and her passing would continue to shape us, as did other successes and tragedies of life. She understood well that her absence in our daily lives would profoundly affect us, her children.

As we had lunch together after the mass and in conversation later, it became clear that Mom's faith, guidance, and humour remain ever-present in our lives. It was akin to when Mom lost something; she would pray three Hail Marys and the missing object reappeared. Of course, it would reappear — she seemed to have her own direct line to God. Our mother was not only blessed but intuitive; in her own patient and mindful way, she had a powerful way of making things work out.

Father Tom performed the mass in memory of Mom. He was the Father who said mass at our Mom's care home. He recalled that she attended religiously and, through his encouragement, she and a few ladies at the care home regularly gathered and prayed the Rosary.

The owner of Mom's care home attended the church where the mass was held. Our family knew her, and the Father also knew her and her family. We have all been connected through Mom. One of my cousins, a Catholic Brother, attended the mass and lunch. He had known Father Tom for many years, so again, we were linked.

While having lunch, we fondly remembered how

we playfully called Mom "Holy Mary." I jokingly asked Father Tom how we could have our Mother, our own "Holy Mary," canonized or be made a saint. He shared his view that everyone in Heaven is just that, a saint. And we said, "There you have it. Our mother IS a Saint!"

Later, I talked with my best friend, Linda, about our incredible day, the beautiful mass and luncheon for my Mom. It felt like my mother was with us in spirit. Like Mom, Linda was a practicing Catholic. She shared with me that May is the "Month of Mary" in the Catholic Church. This was new information for me. However, I am sure Mom was well versed on the Virgin Mary and the Month of May and had subtly led us to find this out at this specific time. Well, thank you, Mom, what a great gift!

As I understand it, May has been dedicated as the Month of Mary since the 13th century. May is the month when spring begins and relates to the renewal of nature. Therefore, May is a perfect month to honour the Virgin Mary, who can be said to have given new life to the world when she birthed Jesus. There are many traditions in May to honour the Virgin Mary. Many parishes have a daily recital of the rosary during May. The rosary has a special prayer dedicated to the Virgin Mary called "Hail Mary." It has been said that there is no problem that the rosary cannot solve. Our mother wholeheartedly believed this to be so. The Catholic church teaches that faithfully praying the Rosary offers protection, answers prayers, and provides mercy and grace. In addition, praying the Rosary will invoke the Virgin Mary's powerful maternal intercession and her virtues of purity, faith, obedience, patience, mercy, charity, humility, and continual prayer. Our mother embodied all these characteristics.

The Virgin Mary has been defined as the "Mother of Mothers," the "Queen of All Saints," and an appropriate role model for women. The Bible, one of our mother's favourite books, often addresses the celebration of motherhood and mothers and honours the Virgin Mary. For Mom, praying the Hail Marys of the rosary was integral to her faith and life. For us, her children, she was our queen, our "Mother of Mothers."

Unrelated to any religion, Mother's Day dates to ancient times. Ancient Greeks, Phrygians, and Romans held celebrations to honour mothering goddesses, practices which continued into medieval times. However, over the centuries, the celebrations diminished until the early 1900s, when there were revivals of festivals in honour of mothers. Thus, Mother's Day was renewed worldwide as a celebration honouring the mother of the family, motherhood, maternal bonds, and the influence of mothers in society — a celebration which takes place in May in most countries and March or the beginning of spring in other countries.

Conventional writings on motherhood identify numerous responsibilities in the role of a mother, including loving unconditionally, nurturing, guiding, correcting, teaching, training, encouraging, caring for, and supporting physically, emotionally, and financially. Mom consistently provided guidance and supported us; you never doubted that she loved you. She was a source of strength, wisdom and a role model for values. I recall asking her how a mom could love another child as much as their first. She replied simply, "There is always more love; there is always more than enough love to go around." Her philosophy of life and her finest qualities were unconditional love with inclusiveness and acceptance.

Although, at times, she voiced her disappointment with our behavior, she rarely became angry. It must have been her Catholic upbringing; you confessed, all was forgiven, and you started over.

Mom would say, "You are my children. No matter how old you are, I love you." She also said, "I can tell them what to do, but they don't always listen. But I love them anyway." She accepted us, our families and extended families for who we were.

Mom welcomed the month of May. She waited

patiently for the crocuses to bloom — the first sign of spring and the reawakening of the earth and warm sun-filled days. For her, it was a time of rebirth and reaffirmation; another cycle of growth and change was beginning, and she welcomed it physically and spiritually. It once meant spring cleaning, garden preparation, planting, opening the doors and windows, letting the warm air in, and sending the kids outside.

As Mom aged gracefully, the month of May became more of a month of renewal and reflection, with the rosary, a powerful sacramental of the Catholic church, guiding her spiritually. It is said that your soul will be saved if you faithfully say the Rosary every day until death. I believe Mom's faithful prayer of the Rosary opened the gates of Heaven and welcomed her to the everlasting life she believed in.

Our mother Mary's earthly life ended in May; she clearly intended to draw us to the virtues of the Virgin Mary and motherhood. Choosing the month of May to leave us, illuminated the power and grace our mother possessed and shared throughout her life. It was comforting to learn about the significance of the Month of Mary and Mother's Day, and upon reflection, I saw that all the pieces fit together with our mother's gentle nudging.

Mom was skillful at subtly weaving things together for the desired result. She was a woman of patience and prayer. She expected results, but they didn't have to be immediate. So, if one came to know and understand certain things at a specific time, that was simply fine... the plan was unfolding as it should.

On the day we honoured her, and reminisced about her life, we realized Mom continues to be with us, forever guiding, opening doors and our hearts, and connecting us with the family and friends who had supported her and our family over the years. She often said, "You never stop being a mother, and it doesn't get better as your children get older. It gets different." For Mom, it all related to her abiding faith, unconditional love of family, and living in the virtues of motherhood.

As children and in adulthood, we all confided in our mother. We were comforted by her wisdom, support, and hugs to move us through our tears. No matter our age, we sought her advice and guidance. She would offer her thoughtful wisdom, and we felt heard; she gave us a new perspective, and that made us ready to face our challenge. As our Mother did, we strive to accept and adapt to change easily and gracefully.

In honour of our mother, Mary, who passed in the month of May, the Catholic Month of Mary, and May the month of Mother's Day, we pay special tribute and acknowledge the significance of her presence in our lives when she was with us and now that she is with us in spirit. *Thank You For Being Our Mother.*

**"There is always more love;
there is always more than enough
love to go around."**

Mary Koczka

Acknowledgements

I am drawn to acknowledge my mother's gentle nudging to write, though I am certain she would be surprised yet humbled that I chose to write about her.

My thanks to my husband Earl, children Corina, Kevin, and Chad, sisters Winnifred and Wanda, and brother Wayne — who gave me insight and support to write about a woman we all loved dearly.

Thank You to my recently-deceased lifelong best friend, Linda, who told me about the significance of the Month of May. She would proudly be helping me share this accomplishment with anyone who would listen.

Thank You to Leslie, one of Mom's real-life angels for guiding and protecting my dear mother in the last few years of her well lived life.

I am grateful to the members of my Writing Circle, who have come to know and love my mother, and have been extremely helpful in assisting me in showing others the mother I know and love. A special thanks to my beta readers: Pat, Beth, Corina, Justin, Madeline, Marion, and Peter.

I have been shaped and influenced by family members who are no longer with me. Even in their absence I hear their words and appreciate our relationships. You were all significant in my life: my grandparents, my dad, my brother Wallace, and my dear friend and family partner, my brother Wes.

I appreciate the encouragement I received from friends and extended family.

To my editor and publisher, Jeanne Martinson, thank you for your invaluable role in bringing this book to life, a labour of love in which I take pride.

If others come to know and be inspired by my mother's journey, I have done what I set out to do. I trust Mom would be pleased with my representation of her life. Someday I hope to receive a sign from my mom, saying, "Well done, Wanita. Well done."

About the Author

Wanita J Koczka, aka WJK3, grew up in Saskatoon, Saskatchewan. She lives on an acreage at the edge of the Boreal Forest near Prince Albert, Saskatchewan. She recently retired from a forty-year career in Corrections management, where she refined her non-fiction writing skills. As the primary caregiver for her elderly mother, who passed during

COVID-19 in 2021, she was moved to give voice to her mother's life through an unconventional memoir. Unlike her Corrections world, her writing in this memoir is rich, emotive, and sprinkled with wit.

Like her mother, Wanita cherishes family time, Christmas, and family celebrations. She is a results-oriented woman who takes pride in her hard work and the value she adds to both her family and work life. Her most significant achievement is earning a Bachelor of Social Work while working full-time and raising three children. It took her ten years of night and summer classes to obtain her degree, which was crucial to her career advancement.

www.ingramcontent.com/pod-product-compliance
Lightning Source LLC
Chambersburg PA
CBHW072115050526
44107CB00098BA/189